Suit Up!

Empowered with Purpose

Suit Up!

Empowered with Purpose

Lillian Laitman

Copyright © 2020 Lillian Laitman
Powered by WoW Media
www.lillianlaitman.com

All rights reserved. No part of this publication may be reproduced, distributed, or transmitted in any form or by any means, including photocopying, recording, or other electronic or mechanical methods, without the prior written permission of the publisher, except in the case of brief quotations embodied in critical reviews and certain other noncommercial uses permitted by copyright law.

For permission requests, contact the publisher at the email, wowmedia19@gmail.com, "Attention: Permissions Coordinator."

Unless otherwise noted, all Scripture quotations are from the Holy Bible, New International Version®, NIV®. Copyright © 1973, 1978, 1984, 2011 by Biblica, Inc.® Used by permission of Zondervan. All rights reserved worldwide. www.zondervan.com. The "NIV" and "New International Version" are trademarks registered in the United States Patent and Trademark Office by Biblica, Inc.®

Scripture quotations marked AMP are from the Amplified Bible. Copyright © 2015 by The Lockman Foundation. Used by permission. www.Lockman.org.

Scripture quotations marked ESV are from the Holy Bible, English Standard Version. Copyright © 2001 by Crossway Bibles, a division of Good News Publishers. Used by permission.

Scripture quotations marked KJV are from the King James Version of the Bible.

Scripture quotations marked NKJV are taken from the New King James Version®. Copyright © 1982 by Thomas Nelson. Used by permission. All rights reserved.

Scripture quotations marked NLT are taken from the Holy Bible, New Living Translation, copyright © 1996, 2004, 2007. Used by permission of Tyndale House Publishers, Inc., Wheaton, IL 60189. All rights reserved.

ISBN: 978-1-7345942-0-1 (Paperback)
ISBN: 978-1-7345942-2-5 (E-Pub)

Cover design by Lisa McClure

Back cover photo credit: Karen Kurta of Karen K Photo

A portion of the proceeds from every copy sold will be donated to Lake Mary Church to assist them in giving back to the local community, the nation, and the world.

Honor God, Love Life, and Make Disciples

1 2 3 4 5 6 7 8 INGS 25 24 23 22 21 20

Dedication

To my love, my best friend, my Lord and Savior, Jesus Christ—You are the only one to never leave me or abandon me and to show me unconditional love, even when I was my most unlovable and didn't deserve it.

To Josefina, or Ma as I called her—She left an indelible impression on everyone she met. She was kindhearted, too trusting at times, and a loving woman. I'm sure she hid her superheroine cape in the house somewhere. I love you, Ma. Thanks for leaving me a legacy of faith that no money on earth can buy. Thank you for your unconditional love, even though I didn't understand just how deep a mother's love runs until I became a mother. As you used to say, "I'll see you in the morning."

To Grandma Julia—She had no more than a third-grade education yet taught herself to read by using the Bible as a textbook. Every day she'd sit in the rocker in our family room and read page after page, then she would follow her reading with a time of prayer. She was the matriarch of our family, and her legacy will continue for generations to come.

To my gifts from God, Connor and Kaitlyn—I am so blessed to be your mom. I'm proud of the people you are transforming into every day. Thank you for supporting me during graduate school, loving me through tough and happy times, and encouraging me to write this book. I love you with all my heart (and all my guts)!

For though we walk in the flesh [as mortal men], we are not carrying on our [spiritual] warfare according to the flesh and using the weapons of man. The weapons of our warfare are not physical [weapons of flesh and blood]. Our weapons are divinely powerful for the destruction of fortresses. We are destroying sophisticated arguments and every exalted and proud thing that sets itself up against the [true] knowledge of God, and we are taking every thought and purpose captive to the obedience of Christ.
—2 Corinthians 10:3-5, AMP

Contents

Acknowledgements 3

Introduction: Time to Suit Up! 5

Chapter 1: Strength Doesn't Always Look Like Wonder Woman 15

Chapter 2: Lasso the Lies with the Truth 27

Chapter 3: Become Bulletproof 43

Chapter 4: Boots on the Ground 69

Chapter 5: Take Up Your Shield 91

Chapter 6: Queen in Training 107

Chapter 7: The god-Killer 125

Conclusion: Will You Answer the Call? 147

Recommended Resources 149

About the Author 150

Endnotes 151

Acknowledgements

I would be remiss if I didn't give a shout-out to those who have poured into my life, touched my heart, and in some way been the reason this book exists. There are too many to list by name, but y'all know who you are!

To my sister, Yvonne, who has been an example to me of courage and strength in the heat of the battle. Thank you for loving me. Muah!

To the only family I've truly known, the Merceds. Regardless of what transpires in our lives, we love each other through all of it.

A la única familia que he conocido y tengo, la familia Merced—no importa que pasa entre nosotros, siempre existe amor.

To my spiritual family, Lake Mary Church and Every Nation campus ministry worldwide—I am so grateful to be part of a beautiful body of believers.

To my "sistas from another mista"—there are too many of you to name, but you are the friends who have lifted me up and stood by me when I needed you most. You are my women warriors whom I know I can call on. Thank you and muah!

A special thanks to Lisa McClure, thank you for lending your talents to create the cover design.

To Isabel Liu, many thanks for building my website and lending your professional skills to help me launch my platform as an author.

And finally, to my Lord and Savior, thank You for trusting me to take this message.

Put on the full armor of God, so that you can take your stand against the devil's schemes. For our struggle is not against flesh and blood, but against the rulers, against the authorities, against the powers of this dark world and against the spiritual forces of evil in the heavenly realms.
—Ephesians 6:11–12

Introduction

Time to Suit Up!

Do you remember the childhood story *The Emperor's New Clothes* by Hans Christian Andersen? If you're a millennial, you may recall instead the Disney™ animated movie *The Emperor's New Groove*. Both have more or less the same storyline—a selfish, vain ruler turns a blind eye to the truth around him until one person causes him to see that everything is not as it appeared.

In some ways, we all bear a resemblance to that clueless ruler. We often wear what we think makes us look our very best, whether it's a smile or a mask so nobody can see the real us. We attempt to hide behind a lie because we're afraid of being rejected when people discover the truth. This notion of hiding our weaknesses instead of identifying them was part of the catalyst that led me to write this book.

I've always been fascinated with the comic book character Wonder Woman. Maybe it's because she's the embodiment of everything I thought I wanted to be someday: strong, independent, a defender of the underdog. She would fight tooth and nail to save the world—and always look good while doing it!

I wanted to be just like that—doing it all and being everything my friends and family needed me to be—but I was falling way short. Then it dawned on me one day: *Wonder Woman is a demigoddess. That means she's not all superhero; she's half human. So she must have some weaknesses. What were they?*

Like Wonder Woman, many women go through life donning a superhero cape, rescuing friends and family and trying to balance all the demands that daily living brings. But the reality is that we're not superheroes. Humans have faults and weaknesses; after all, nobody's perfect.

As Christians, we tend to forget that we can tap into powerful weapons that give us supernatural strength. Those weapons allow us to fight the battles we face both in the natural world and in the spiritual realm.

Yet instead of donning those weapons, we try to juggle life ourselves, thinking we can do it all, have it all, and give our all to those we love. But when any of life's challenging moments come up—and they will—this type of invincible mentality only leaves us exposed to attacks on our character because we're human.

When situations don't turn out as we had hoped, the outcome can leave us feeling defeated and hopeless. We need to change our gear and begin wearing the armor God has given us so we can regain the strength to fight bravely for our loved ones and discover all that God intends for us to achieve in this life. (See 2 Samuel 10:12.)

Get Dressed for Battle

For many years I tried to do everything in my own strength. I always thought that if I approached life in a certain way, then everything would just fall into place. That's where my attempt to live in my own strength began to fail. I was trying to fix problems with my own knowledge. I was trying to fix people, thinking I could rescue them, but I'm not supposed to fix anyone. I was focused on "keeping it all together," but in reality things were falling apart.

I had lost hope and peace, and I felt defeated. Then it hit me: the reason things were falling apart was there was too much *I* in the mix. I was professing to be a Christian yet falling short when it came to activating my faith that God could pull me through life's tough situations. I wasn't dressed properly when confronted with life's battles. I was relying too much on the power of a fallible trinity: me, myself, and I.

Over time, God began to deal with my heart and mind, revealing to me how to properly suit up in His armor in order to deal with everyday struggles, and how to wield the spiritual weapons He had already freely given to me.

It was out of personal experience that God began to speak to me about the need for His daughters to properly suit up. The burden to write this book became so strong, I started jotting down ideas as the thoughts came. But because of fear of the unknown and fear of what people might think, I put the book-writing down—for almost five years.

Over the course of my publishing career, I've book-doctored, edited, and ghostwritten many manuscripts, but I allowed fear to keep me from writing my own book. I didn't revisit the idea of finishing this book until a dear friend of mine sent me a text message one day:

> A few days ago, God told me to tell you to start writing something that He told you to write a long time ago. That is what He wants you to do… it's what He has for you.

I saved that message on my cell phone. I carry

Introduction

it everywhere with me as a reminder that God loves me enough to send someone who knew *nothing* of what was on my heart to encourage me to continue the work He assigned me to do.

When I started the journey of penning this book, I never dreamed I would go through all that I did or that each experience would serve as a basis for the inspirational message I hope you find within these pages. I am by no means a scholar; I'm not an ordained minister, theologian, or popular conference speaker. I am *human*. I have flaws just like everyone else. Writing this book is out of my comfort zone because I will be transparent about the lessons I've learned in hopes that they will lift your faith and inspire you to continue moving toward your God-given purpose.

But please don't get me wrong: I certainly don't think I have "arrived" or that I'm better than anyone else. Anybody who makes you feel inferior in any way is full of a whole lot of crapola. Growing spiritually is an open-ended process—you keep learning, stretching, and growing.

There's a reason you picked up this book, and I'm glad you did! My prayer is that as you read these pages, you will learn how to dress for the inner battles you face on a regular basis and how to wield the spiritual weapons given to daughters of the King.

Some people speak of good and bad karma, yin and yang, or good and bad vibes. I call these forces spiritual warfare, and winning these battles requires specialized weapons. The Bible says:

> For though we live in the world, we do not wage war as the world does. The weapons we fight with are not the weapons of the world. On the contrary, they have divine power to demolish strongholds. We demolish arguments and every pretension that sets itself up against the knowledge of God, and we take captive every thought to make it obedient to Christ.
> —2 Corinthians 10:3–6

Look closer at verses 3 and 4: we live in this world, but we don't wage war the same way. Our weapons are not of this world; they have divine power to demolish strongholds. The Greek word translated "demolish" in this passage is *kathairesis,* which means *to take down, destroy, or raze.*[1] Yes, you need to dress for battle so you can raze hell! It's time for you to destroy the weapons of this present world that try to bring you down and possess all that God has promised you—life, peace, and joy, just to name a few of His blessings.

Introduction

The Information Warfare Plan

Modern military tactics include a strategy called *information warfare,* which has been defined as *"any action to deny, exploit, corrupt, or destroy the enemy's information and its functions; protecting ourselves against those actions; and exploiting our own military information functions."*[2] As we discover how to properly suit up for the battles we face, we must also learn how to jam the enemy's lines of communication to our hearts and minds.

This is why at the end of each chapter, you will find an Information Warfare Plan that includes a daily Scripture verse and a focal point based upon the chapter's weapon. When we read God's Word, it becomes a powerful weapon to combat the enemy's strategy to deceive us. Prayer is also a powerful weapon in our arsenal because when we speak God's Word aloud through prayer, it activates our faith and shuts down the enemy's communication strategy.

I recommend that you take your time digesting the information in each chapter. The Scriptures provided at the end are one week's worth of verses carefully chosen so you can meditate and digest the Word of God. Instead of rushing onto the next chapter, take time daily to read the recommended Scripture, meditate on it, pray over it, journal about what God speaks to your heart, and then when you've read all of them, move on to the next chapter.

Although I don't provide you with sample prayers in this book, prayer is critical to our victory. Prayer isn't something we limit to once a week at church, or even once day when we get up in the morning. We should pray *all day, every day.* Prayer isn't just kneeling down for hours at a time. There are many ways you can pray. You can be driving and praying (with your eyes open!). Or you can pray a "bullet prayer"— a quick, targeted prayer—as the Holy Spirit guides you in what or who to pray for. In whatever manner you pray, the key is that you pray. There is power in prayer, whether spoken aloud or in silence. More about prayer later in the book, though.

For now, let's dive in and look at some of the weak spots in Wonder Woman's arsenal and the spiritual weapons at our disposal.

*Therefore, put on the full
armor of God, so that
when the day of evil comes,
you may be able to stand your
ground, and after you have
done everything, to stand.*
—Ephesians 6:13

Chapter 1

Strength Doesn't Always Look Like Wonder Woman

When I was growing up in the 1970s, superheroes were popular, much like they are today. I remember watching Batman, Batgirl, Superman, and the Incredible Hulk on TV, but my personal favorite was Wonder Woman. An Amazonian princess who was said to be the daughter of Zeus, Wonder Woman was blessed with amazing superhuman abilities.

Those powers were on full display in the 1970s TV show *Wonder Woman,* starring Lynda Carter as Diana Prince/Wonder Woman. Carter would spin to transform into Wonder Woman and take out the bad guy singlehandedly—without getting even a hair out of place and with her go-go boots still intact! I loved it.

I remember coming home from school and sitting on the shag rug in our basement in front of our Zenith color television to watch Diana Prince fly around in her invisible jet, saving the world. *Bam! Wham! Pow!* Wonder Woman always caught the criminal. But what was so cool about Wonder Woman wasn't her superpowers but her love for the people she defended. She was tough when she needed to be, yet she had a kind, loving heart. I used to want to be just like her when I grew up.

Oftentimes kids (and even some adults) live in a fantasy world, especially when it comes to superheroes. Their favorite superhero is incapable of failing—ever—because, well, he or she is a superhero. Kids don't rationalize that superheroes are often half-human and have some weakness that their archenemies know how to exploit. As an example, for Superman, it's kryptonite. But I'd never really thought about Wonder Woman's weaknesses…until God gave me the idea to write this book.

In the DC Comics™ storyline, Wonder Woman is a demigod who has superhuman powers and supernatural weapons given to her by the gods to fight her battles. Her archenemies know that if they can pinpoint her weak spots, they can use her own weapons and strength to attack her where she's most vulnerable.

You and I aren't superheroes, but too often we rely on our own strength to get through life's struggles, and our strength inevitably falters in the heat of battle.

However, we have a heavenly Father who has given us what we need to win the fight. We just need to suit up and learn how to engage our enemy in battle.

> *When someone tells you that you can't, turn around and say, "Watch me."*
> *—Anonymous*

I'm talking about a spiritual battle, and if we want to have a stormproof (not storm-free) life, we need to equip ourselves.

Wonder Woman's Weak Spots

In this book, I'll use some of Wonder Woman's weak spots as analogies of humanistic strength and contrast them with our God-given weapons. I'll unpack for you the truth of God's Word about the power that's available to you to build a stormproof life (Eccl. 12:10).

In researching Wonder Woman's weaknesses, I discovered a source that outlines fifteen of them.[1] (Who knew!) For the sake of my analogy, I'm listing six of her weapons in this section, which is followed by a section that lists our God-given weapons as found in Ephesians 6.

Weapon	How It's Used Against Her
Lasso of Truth	"Mostly known for its ability to force the truth out of someone, it can also trap people of various strength levels. Basically a God-like weapon, even Wonder Woman has fallen victim to it by being trapped by the lasso. Normally, people assume that the lasso is built on Diana's own emotions and desires and thus being trapped by it is impossible, but for some reason over the years…she has fallen victim to it. The truth being forced out of her with it has not been a huge success, though."
Bracelets of Submission[2]	"The bracelets are actually power inhibitors. They are basically made to keep Diana's powers down to a manageable level. She is already amazingly powerful, has super speed, and can fly. And that's not even to mention her tactical advantages having grown up learning from the Amazons. Without the bracelets, though, her power grows in a massive way, which means one of her most notable uniform attachments are actually hindering her from using her full power."
Shield	There is no known basis for her shield being used as a weapon against her.

Piercing Weapons (e.g., spear, arrow)	"One of the many things seen with the Amazons is old school weapons like spears and arrows. Both of these are used by Wonder Woman in her training, which is essential to all who wish to call themselves a true warrior of the Amazons.... Several times throughout the comics Wonder Woman has been seen bleeding... [because she] is not completely immortal, in fact... her human side can be hurt."
Tiara	Her Amazonian crown, the Tiara of Themyscira, is used as a boomerang to deter enemies. Like most of her supernatural weapons, if it were destroyed—in this case, melted—she could lose her supernatural abilities.
Sword, the god-Killer	The Flashing Blade, also called the god-killer, may be one of the most fearsome weapons in all of DC Comics™. "One of the blade's many powers is the ability subdue its victims, but Nemesis [a goddess charged with bringing death upon those who commit unjust murder] uses the blade's true potential and siphons Wonder Woman's powers into herself. Eventually Wonder Woman regains her strength and defeats Nemesis by wielding the Flashing Blade against her."

The Armor of God Is Our Strength

As women, we often wear many different hats. On the job, we may be supervising a team of coworkers. We deal with the daily stressors of meeting goals and dodging office politics in addition to being overburdened with heavy workloads. At home, we take care of family members—our spouse, maybe children, aging parents, or extended family who need our support. We also are responsible for grocery shopping, cooking, cleaning, paying bills, doing laundry, and the list goes on. In the community, we may be committed to our local church, nonprofit organizaitons, or involved in extracurricular activities.

It's exhausting just reading it!

For these reasons it's important we learn to walk daily in our God-given strength. Walking around in our own strength, which hasn't been proven in the fire and whose mettle hasn't been tested, leaves us vulnerable to attack and exposes our weaknesses, as in the case of my superhero, Wonder Woman.

The Bible warns us to be wary of the enemy's fiery arrows. It also says, "For the weapons of our warfare are not carnal but mighty in God for pulling down strongholds, casting down arguments and every high thing that exalts itself against the knowledge of God, bringing every thought into captivity to the obedience of Christ" (2 Cor. 10:4–5, NKJV).

Each chapter in this book will show you how to dress for battle in this unseen armor. There would appear to be six pieces of armor, which I outline in the following table.

Weapon	Its Purpose
Belt of truth	Holds everything together and points to the fact that we need to be grounded in the truth of God's Word.
Breastplate of righteousness	Guards our heart, the seat of our emotions, and reminds us that pursuing His righteousness helps us avoid sin.
Shoes of peace	Help us to assume a "ready stance" and fight for what we know is true; also help us be prepared to share God's Word with others.
Shield of faith	Blocks the enemy's fiery darts against attacks on our mind; shows that having a solid faith in God keeps us on course even in the middle of a battle.
Helmet of salvation	No head, we're dead! Indicates that without salvation, there is no life in the Spirit.

Sword of the Spirit—God's Word	a) The only offensive weapon on this list; reminds us that we must be grounded in God's Word to fight temptation and spiritual attacks. b) Once we've read the Word and digested it into our spirit, we should verbalize it in prayer so that it becomes activated through our profession of faith.

This entire book is based upon this passage from Ephesians 6:

> Finally, be strong in the Lord and in his mighty power. Put on the full armor of God, so that you can take your stand against the devil's schemes. For our struggle is not against flesh and blood, but against the rulers, against the authorities, against the powers of this dark world and against the spiritual forces of evil in the heavenly realms. Therefore put on the full armor of God, so that when the day of evil comes, you may be able to stand your ground, and after you have done everything, to stand. Stand firm then, with the belt of truth buckled around your waist, with the breastplate of

> righteousness in place, and with your feet fitted with the readiness that comes from the gospel of peace. In addition to all this, take up the shield of faith, with which you can extinguish all the flaming arrows of the evil one. Take the helmet of salvation and the sword of the Spirit, which is the word of God. And pray in the Spirit on all occasions with all kinds of prayers and requests. With this in mind, be alert and always keep on praying for all the Lord's people.
> —Ephesians 6:10–18

If you go back and read the first half of the chapter, you'll see the apostle Paul outlined our responsibilities for each relationship in life, from our children to our parents to our employees or employers. Then in verse 10 he says, "Finally, be strong in the Lord and in his mighty power."

We need to learn to balance all of our relationships because each person who enters our lives is there for a reason. People don't enter our lives by accident. There's a reason our worlds have collided. There is something only *you* can offer that others need to experience. Through our gifts and talents, we can live life out loud for God.

It can be draining on a person emotionally, physically, financially, and spiritually to rely on their own knowledge and strength. That's why the apostle Paul exhorts the Ephesians by saying, "*Finally*, be strong in the Lord." Nobody can go through life trying to have a work-life balance without God's strength and without being properly prepared for the daily battles they will face. If we continue to operate in our own strength and our own understanding, we will fall. Notice I said *fall*, not *fail*. At some point we all fail, because we're human. (See Romans 3:23.)

Information Warfare Plan

As you study this week's scriptures, think about what each piece of armor signifies to you. Journal what the Holy Spirit reveals to you during your quiet time.

Recommended Daily Scriptures:

- Day 1: Ephesians 6:10–11
- Day 2: Ephesians 6:12
- Day 3: Ephesians 6:13
- Day 4: Ephesians 6:14
- Day 5: Ephesians 6:15
- Day 6: Ephesians 6:16–17
- Day 7: Ephesians 6:18

*Stand firm then, with
the belt of truth buckled
around your waist.*

—Ephesians 6:14

Chapter 2

Lasso the Lies with the Truth

Wonder Woman's Lasso of Truth is probably her most notable weapon. It compels anyone who is bound by its power to obey the wielder of the lasso and speak the truth. In the 2017 *Wonder Woman* movie, there's a scene where American pilot Steve Trevor arrives in Themyscira during World War II and is brought before Hippolyta, queen of the Amazons and mother of Diana/Wonder Woman. As the Amazonian women begin to interrogate him, the golden lasso glows brighter and hotter when Steve lies or tells half-truths. Eventually, they get him to confess that the German army is nearby, posing grave danger to their existence. Some comic storylines have chronicled that even Wonder Woman was forced to submit to the lasso's power, although it didn't last on her.[1]

I find it fitting that the first piece of spiritual armor listed in Ephesians 6 is the belt of truth, because John 14:6 says Jesus is "the way, the truth, and the life" (NKJV). In Roman times, the belt played a critical role in the effectiveness of a soldier's armor. The belt was where the soldier placed his sword. Without the belt, he could be missing his most important weapon. For believers, the belt holds the sword of the Spirit, linking the truth and God's Word (John 17:17). Without understanding what truth is, we can easily be deceived (Eph. 4:14). And deception is the enemy's overarching counter-weapon to the belt of truth.

God desires truth—sincerity—in the most inward parts of our lives (Ps. 51:6). When we act with sincere hearts, walking in truth and integrity, we can stand strong. Many who don't follow God or have a relationship with Him will note what Christians do wrong because they know we're held to a higher standard. Does being a Christian mean we don't fall, make mistakes, or sometimes stumble in our truth-walk? Not at all. We are human, after all. We're not infallible or invincible like comic book superheroes, but we can make a daily effort to walk in truth and integrity. Doing the right thing even when nobody is watching—that's integrity. With every step we take to walk a path of truth, we strengthen our resolve to do the right thing. And in so doing, we don't leave ourselves exposed to the enemy attacking our character.

Other People's Perception of You Is *Not* Reality

Oftentimes as women, we mistake someone's perception of us as reality, as if their opinion of us is truth. That kind of lie can be damaging to a woman's self-worth and self-confidence, distorting the truth of who she really is.

I went to a networking event once and met a highly intelligent young woman who was studying to become a medical professional. We exchanged the usually small talk at these types of events, but our conversation turned deeper when I began to share the vision for this book. When I explained how I came up with the concept, she was fascinated and said the message resonated with her. This was not only because she was a young woman seeking to advance her career, but also because she felt the message could help her younger sister in grade school.

As our conversation continued, this young woman unburdened her concern for her little sister's mental health. The pressure of measuring up and constantly comparing herself to others had left the younger sister in a fragile state of mind. My heart ached as I sensed the young lady's desperate cry for something that would help her sister see the truth—the truth that she didn't need to compare herself to any of the girls in her school. She is a beautiful little girl with her whole life yet to live.

That's when I shared with her the truth about others' perception of us. Their perception is not reality; it's simply their perception, and we don't have to buy into it! Each person is created with a unique purpose that only she can fulfill.

The source of truth is Jesus Christ because He *is the truth.* Jesus said, "I am the way *and the truth* and the life. No one comes to the Father except through me" (John 14:6, emphasis added). And in coming to know Jesus on a personal level, you begin to understand He is the truth who sets you free from the shackles of sin and the burdens this world piles on your shoulders.

> *Then you will know the truth,*
> *and the truth will set you free.*
> *—John 8:32*

What I've learned in life is the direction we take in our relationship with Christ impacts our perception of the truth. For instance, during the times I drifted away from Christ, my perception of the truth became distorted by what the circumstances I was facing in that period dictated. In contrast, for each step I took toward a closer relationship with Christ, a more accurate perception of who I really am began to emerge. I saw and understood that I am deeply loved. I am beautiful in God's eyes. I am unique.

In drawing closer to the Living Truth—Jesus Christ—the desire to compare to others faded because my self-perception changed. I understood I was uniquely and wonderfully fashioned to be me, and He loves me just the way I am!

There is an outright attack on the emotional, mental, and spiritual wellbeing of girls in middle and high school, and it continues into college. So many girls and young women feel pressured through social media and society to look a certain way, act a certain way, or be at a certain social status. Why? They are being attacked by an enemy called *comparison*.

Lots of women—young and old—have bought into the lies comparison whispers in their ears rather than standing on the truth of who their Creator made them to be! As the mom of a daughter in this critical age group, I never imagined how intensely my daughter would have to battle these attacks on her self-worth and wellbeing daily. Even with the love, support, and spiritual guidance of her family, it's still tough. Most of the girls—especially during their middle school years—have to battle the pull to constantly compare themselves to their peers. They ask themselves, "How come her hair is so silky straight and mine is curly? Why is she developing faster than I am? How does she eat so much and stay so thin? Why are these girls so mean to me? I feel so ugly. I wish I was (fill in the blank)."

For most girls, the comparison is coming from a need to belong and be desired by boys. Hormones are raging! But comparison is the enemy of joy.

> *Comparison is the enemy of joy.*

The effect of comparison on a young woman's life hit my local community hard. A young lady at a local high school was going through some difficult times. Her mother was not around for reasons unknown, leaving her father to raise her by himself. The parents were from another country, so there was racial prejudice to confront. Although she was a beautiful, exotic-looking girl, she only saw her flaws. And then there were guy troubles and social media bullying to deal with. For whatever reason, everything culminated with this young lady ending her life. Our pastors led a "celebration of life" in the school auditorium that overflowed with people—young, old, peers, teachers, community workers, and people who didn't know her at all, like me.

I remember sitting in the very last row of the packed room listening to people share all the wonderful things this young woman did—how she had touched people's lives with her personality, her music, her love for drawing. She will never know how much she was truly loved—so much that even complete strangers came to show their support and pay their respects. I sobbed until the makeup ran down my face.

The compassion I felt for her father and loved ones made my heart ache. To think that she was so loved and was completely overcome by the lies of her enemy, comparison, instead of believing the truth. She touched so many in the short time she was here on earth, and she'll never know the void she leaves in hearts of those who knew her. She lacked the strength to see beyond the pain of the now-moment and recognize the potential within her.

Truth: Your Enemies Are Invisible

Another lie we need to lasso with the truth: people are not our enemies; the true enemy is not of this world. In the movie *The Nutty Professor 2,* there's a scene in which Professor Klump's grandmother and father begin arguing in the church. The grandmother turns to the professor's father and says, "I'd like to choke the life out of you right there in front of Jesus!" It's funny! But if we are truly honest, who hasn't felt like that about someone at some point in their lives. This is not exactly a good example of godly character but it's human nature to sometimes become so exasperated with people to lose sight of the truth.

The truth is that the people who seem to constantly come against us are not our enemies. We have an unseen enemy who has a vast army of demons with rank but limited powers. Charismatic believers have a saying, "new levels, new devils." I don't know where the saying originated from but Ephesians 6:12 highlights that there are demonic influences at different levels in the spiritual realm. There are: "rulers," "authorities," "powers," and "spiritual forces." I encourage you to read Daniel 10. Daniel was fasting and praying, and an angel from heaven was dispatched to help him but was detained by "the prince of the Persian kingdom" (vs. 13). Then who else can match an evil principality but Michael, the archangel, to knock out that evil prince! (vs. 14).

No doubt our conversations and decisions take place in the physical realm; yet, what transpires from those conversations and decisions impact the spiritual realm. Until we realize the truth that our enemy is not a physical person but a spiritual being, we will continue to look for physical solutions to solve spiritual problems manifesting themselves in our physical lives.

> *Until we realize the truth that our enemy is not a physical person but a spiritual being, we will continue to look for physical solutions to solve spiritual problems manifesting themselves in our physical lives.*

Personally, I've come to realize the greatest battles happen when: (1) I let my spiritual guard down; (2) I'm not focusing on God's Word and praying; (3) I stop connecting with my church family; (4) I'm physically and emotionally exhausted.

Our battle is not against our neighbor, spouse, coworker, child, or even our own propensities or weaknesses in our flesh. (See Ephesians 6:12.) People are simply a conduit for the spiritual battle taking place in another realm—the heavens. The "heavens" simply means in the spiritual realm.

As we continue our daily walk of faith, realize that people are not our enemy. Our task is to see past their actions and ask God to guide us in discerning the spiritual situation.

Truth and Consequences

As a little girl, I used to lie all the time to my mom to avoid facing her wrath. Yet Mom had a lot of wisdom and wasn't about to let me pull the wool over eyes. I recall one time in particular when I tried lying to her about something. She saw right through me (maybe I looked guilty) and said, "I can always tell when you're lying because one eye turns green and the other eye turns light brown." Mom didn't need Wonder Woman's iconic golden lasso to compel me to tell the truth. She knew just what to say, but I didn't know what she was doing.

The next time I lied to her and was confronted, I asked her, "OK, so what color are my eyes now?" She laughed so hard, and I couldn't for the life of me understand why she thought my question was so funny. Ah, childhood memories.

As a child, I avoided the truth, but as an adult, I've learned that the truth is one of our most important pieces of spiritual armor. We may not possess a truth lasso like Wonder Woman's that we can use to compel people to tell us the truth, but we can hold fast to the truth.

God doesn't always save us from our foolish decisions. Our choices—good or bad, right or wrong—are our own. Some might argue, "Well, if He's such a loving God, then why doesn't He stop people from doing bad things or making bad choices?" My response is, He's not out to manipulate us like puppets.

I'm reminded of a discussion I had with a friend over this subject. His earliest experience of faith was growing up in the Catholic church, which he deeply resented and equated that childhood experience with a vengeful God. During our conversation, he asked me, "So if God is so good, then tell me why is there so much evil in this world and bad things happening to innocent people? Why does God allow it?"

I looked him squarely in the eyes and said, "You have children. Do you love your children?"

With a puzzled look, he responded, "Of course!"

"Do you want the best for your children?"

Again, perplexed by my question and a bit annoyed he responded, "Most definitely."

"If you see any of your children going down a wrong path or making poor choices, do you manipulate them to make good choices or take the path of least resistance?"

He thought and responded, "As much as it would hurt me to see them make a mistake, I would never manipulate them."

I responded, "If you wouldn't manipulate your children into making right choices to avoid negative consequences, then much less does God manipulate us regarding the choices we make."

Any parent knows that you can try to help your child see what lies ahead, but ultimately, the child must make his own choices and face the consequences. As a parent, you hope a lesson is learned if a wrong choice is made.

Throughout Scripture, God lets His children make wrong choices and suffer the consequences. We see that when Abraham and Sarah tried to help God fulfill His promise to them by having Abraham bear a son with Sarah's handmaid Hagar. God still gave Abraham and Sarah the child He promised, but the strife between the descendants of Hagar's son, Ishmael, and Sarah's son, Isaac, continues to plague the Middle East to this day.

God will allow us to make foolish decisions or take matters into our own hands. He has given us free will, but that doesn't mean we are free from the consequences. And many times, those consequences are ongoing. Does that mean God doesn't love us or is somehow punishing us? Not at all. Look at what Psalm 103:11–13 says:

> For as high as the heavens are above the earth, so great is his love for those who fear him; as far as the east is from the west, so far has he removed our transgressions from us. As a father has compassion on his children,

so the Lord has compassion on those
who fear him.

God allows consequences because He is holy and because He loves us so much. We can't disobey Him and "get away with it." At some point, the consequences catch up with us, but God still loves us before, during, and after our foolish decisions.

Take, for example, David and Bathsheba. David had an affair with Bathsheba, who eventually became pregnant with a son. When David found out, he tried to get Bathsheba's husband, Uriah, to sleep with his wife, but Uriah, a soldier, refused to rest at home while his fellow soldiers were in battle. So David plotted to have Uriah killed in battle. The consequence of David's decision was great. David and Bathsheba's firstborn child died. God didn't just leave a consequence, though. Instead, God showed David mercy after he repented. David and Bathsheba later had a son named Solomon, who became one of the great kings of Israel. On top of that, Jesus was born out of his lineage.

So do we keep on sinning and expect a future blessing? Absolutely not. That would be playing with fire and directly challenging God. Remember, God is holy. Yes, He is merciful, but He also weighs the intentions of our heart and wants us to willingly obey Him.

Is there any area in your life where you recognize you may not be fully obeying God? Why not take the steps necessary to get right with Him? Run back to Abba Father today and ask for a fresh start. He's waiting to show you His mercy.

Never look for an easy way out of any situation that is attempting to knock you out. Do whatever you can to pave a path to God and the life He wants for you. Yes, it will be difficult, but it's always rewarding to trust God as He equips you to set goals for your life. And God has gifted many professionals—doctors, counselors, pastors, teachers/professors, physical therapists, personal trainers, and so on—with the wisdom to help people reach their goals.

Gird Your Loins!

One of my favorite novels is *The Devil Wears Prada,* about a young woman who becomes the assistant for a very difficult fashion magazine editor. In one scene, to warn the staff that their boss is arriving earlier than expected, a character named Nyles yells, "Everyone! Gird your loins!" In other words, brace yourself for a dangerous situation.

I'm calling on you to gird your loins, to tighten your belt of truth—that is, the truth of who God says who you are. It's time for you to believe the truth of who you were created to be and walk in the strength of that knowledge.

There are people you will reach that I can never reach, people whose lives you will enrich in a special way. I don't have that superpower—*you do,* because only you can reach them! The truth is that within each one of us lies the power of the Holy Spirit who endows us with special gifts to be used to help those within our sphere of influence and help us in our time of need.

Stop comparing yourself and stop buying into the lie that you are who people perceive you to be. Those perceptions don't define who you were created to be and what you were created to do. Be yourself and fulfill your purpose. There are people counting on you.

Information Warfare Plan

As you meditate on this week's scriptures, reflect on what these verses declare to be truth in your life.

Recommended Daily Scriptures:

- Day 1: Psalm 119:160
- Day 2: Ephesians 4:21–25
- Day 3: John 8:32
- Day 4: Deuteronomy 28:13
- Day 5: 1 John 1:5–9
- Day 6: Psalm 145
- Day 7: Proverbs 14:1–7

Stand firm then...with the breastplate of righteousness in place.
—Ephesians 6:14

Chapter 3

Become Bulletproof

Like her lasso, Wonder Woman's bracelets are one of the most defining parts of her outfit. But they are actually a weakness for her. Yes, they can be used to deflect bullets or any other projectiles, but the bracelets are actually power inhibitors.[1] Wonder Woman is amazingly strong, has super speed, and can fly. And that doesn't even include her combat training as an Amazonian princess. Yet left unchecked, her powers would be too strong for her to control. So those bracelets keep Wonder Woman's strengths down to a manageable level.

But that's not the only purpose for the bracelets. In an interview, William Moulton Marston, creator of the superhero character, said the bracelets were meant to remind Wonder Woman and the Amazonians of their past enslavement to Greek men. Later, Aphrodite (the goddess of love) would free the Amazonian women, but they would wear the bracelets as a reminder to never surrender their power to any man.[2]

In a similar way, as women we are sensitive to emotions—both our own and others'—and if left unchecked, this "superpower" will lead us into a form of bondage to our feelings. We have a choice to either become enslaved to our emotions or protect the seat of our emotions—our hearts—by living a righteous life.

Being righteous doesn't mean we're more "holy" or better than anyone else; our good deeds are "as filthy rags" (Isa. 64:6, KJV). Our righteousness is given to us by a holy God; He alone is righteous. When we learn to wear His righteousness and give Jesus control over our hearts and emotions, then He can protect us from things that deeply wound our souls, including emotions such as condemnation, low self-esteem, depression, fear, anxiety, unforgiveness, and resentment. In a sense, we can become bulletproof.

The Battles Women Face

In the 2017 movie *Wonder Woman,* Diana comes face-to-face with Ares, the god of war, on a tarmac, where they duke it out. It's one of the more intense scenes in the film, as the battle between good and evil reaches its height. But if you really analyze the scene, there's a moral in there. Diana's love for Steve Trevor and for mankind are what compel her to fight for justice.

The other interesting twist in this scene is the battle itself. Their fight goes beyond the physical confrontation; it's also a battle of the mind. Ares continually bombards Diana with negative thoughts, trying to convince her to give up on mankind and making her feel as if the situation is hopeless because man is beyond redemption. And for a brief moment, Diana struggles with entertaining the thought as if it were the truth, but it's not. Ultimately, she chooses to believe that love can overcome even the worst situation.

This is what the enemy does to us. His attacks aren't physical. If they were, it would be easier to guard against them. No, the enemy's chief method of moving you outside of your purpose is by attacking your soul, which is the seat of your mind, will, and emotions. (Bible teacher Joyce Meyer talks about this in her book *The Battlefield of the Mind*, which I highly recommend.) There are two common types of attack on your soul:

1. **Mental attacks:** The devil attacks the mind and begins to twist your thoughts and perspective in order to bring confusion. Satan's mental attacks can leave you feeling paralyzed in your thought life and bewildered.
2. **Pressure:** This tactic is a lead

> indicator of a demonic plot. The kingdom of God is full of power and authority—but not pressure. The Holy Spirit leads you (Rom. 8:14); He does not force you or intimidate you into being obedient. Those are tactics of your enemy.

As we saw in the previous chapter, strapping ourselves spiritually with the truth of God's Word is critical in spiritual warfare. If we're not careful and allow some version of the truth to be distorted, our misperceptions can lead us to compromise what we know to be right.

In the sections that follow, we'll take a look at some emotions that the enemy exploits to derail us from our purpose, including:

- Low self-esteem
- Loneliness
- Anxiety
- Unforgiveness
- Rejection

By exposing how the enemy uses these negative emotions against us, we can make our hearts bulletproof and, as a result, do what is right in God's eyes.

Know Who You Are

Most women who struggle with self-esteem issues often feel as if they don't measure up to a certain standard. Low self-esteem is an emotion that the enemy uses against us to mask the truth of who God says we are.

As a kid, I was bullied throughout grade school. In elementary school, I was teased a lot for being overweight. In middle school, I "blossomed" faster than most girls at that age and was teased mercilessly by boys and girls alike. I had no self-esteem because I believed the negative words that had been spoken against me were true. Then as I matured emotionally and spiritually, I began to make my heart bulletproof by believing what God had to say about me. I battled to overcome these negative thoughts by reminding myself that I was so special to God that the very hairs on my head are numbered (Luke 12:7), and that I'm unique and wonderfully made (Ps. 139:13). Knowing who I am in Him has helped strengthen my resolve to stand for what is right, regardless of what society may try to impose on me.

The key to our emotional stability is knowing who we are in Christ. It's how we will break away from old patterns of shame-based thinking and the caustic habit of trying harder and getting nowhere. We are the head and not the tail (Deut. 28:13). We are the apple of our Father's eye as Psalm 17:8 says, hidden in the shadow of His wings and dressed in the royalty of His favor.

Knowing our worth to God is the first step toward personal change. In Jesus we become *new* people, someone we have never been previously (2 Cor. 5:17). We are not who we used to be; we are much more! Neither our past nor what others say about us defines who we are.

How would your actions change if you saw yourself as a world-changer? How would it affect every person with whom you came into contact? Think about that. If your enemy can wage war in your mind to lower your self-esteem and trap you into believing you are less than who you really are, then he wins. If you can combat those negative thoughts and verbally confess the exact opposite, then you gain the upper hand against your enemy.

There's Only One Who Satisfies

Loneliness—that feeling of separation or lack of companionship—is another emotion the enemy exploits to attack us. Loneliness is something anyone can relate to regardless of whether they're single, married, young, or old. Some people can be in a crowded room and still feel lonely. Shortly after my divorce, I was faced with the painful realization at night that there was no other adult in the house with whom I could share all that transpired during the day or who could lend me support if something happened with the kids.

Many believe that if they only had a spouse, their loneliness would go away. Although it might take the edge off the discomfort, the deepest longing of the heart is communion with God. What would happen if we saw loneliness as a good thing? What if instead of running from loneliness in pursuit of another relationship, we ran to Jesus, asking Him to fill the void? What if we remembered that just as physical solitude enables us to hear the Father's voice, inner solitude enables us to know the Father's character as our comforter, companion, and sustainer?

I grew up in a single parent household, so I never knew what it was to see my parents interact on a daily basis. And I was the only child because my siblings were much older and weren't living at home. I adapted to my surroundings, but deep down I always wanted to know what it was like to have a dad in the house. I longed for what I thought was that sense of security until I matured and realized God strengthens the alienated at heart. David proclaimed, "Even if my father and mother abandon me, the Lord will hold me close" (Ps. 27:10, NLT). I memorized this verse in my early teens to protect my heart from the perception of loneliness and feelings of abandonment by an absent father.

Maybe you feel isolated and alone. Know this: you're never closer to God than when you're standing in the darkness. That is when He is closest to you. In what ways are you asking the Father to "hold you close"?

Our heavenly Father promises in Hebrews 13:5, "Never will I leave you; never will I forsake you." The dictionary defines the word *never* as "not in any degree: not under any condition."[3] It's an adverb, which describes an action.

In one of his sermons my pastor unpacked the meaning of the word *never* within the context of Hebrews 13:5, which reads this way in the Amplified Bible.

> Let your character [your moral essence, your inner nature] be free from the love of money [shun greed—be financially ethical], being content with what you have; for He has said, "I *will never [under any circumstances] desert you [nor give you up nor leave you without support, nor will I in any degree leave you helpless], nor will I forsake or*

> *let you down or relax My hold on you [assuredly not]!"*
> —Hebrews 13:5, emphasis added

Basically, my pastor shared that the first half of the statement—"never will I leave you"—signified that God promised He would never abandon us in a physical sense. Although we often feel lonely, we're never truly alone because He's constantly with us. The second half—"never will I forsake you"—signifies that God will never emotionally abandon us. How powerful a thought, especially for women who crave emotional intimacy! He is a father to the fatherless and a defender of widows (Ps. 68:5).

Don't allow loneliness to penetrate your heart and cause you to believe the lie that you're alone. No other person will ever fulfill your heart's desires the way God can. Even at your lowest point, His love for you remains unchanged. When you learn to believe and accept that, you'll finally experience the love and belonging you've been searching for.

Cast All Your Anxiety on Him

Some of us have experienced traumatic events that left us with feelings of anxiety. Often things happen that we can't control or predict, causing anxiety attacks, which is one of the worst feelings ever! An anxiety attack can feel like a heart attack, except it's debilitating both physically and emotionally.

If you've ever experienced anxiety, you're not alone and you're not crazy. It comes as a result of trying to shield yourself from further emotional harm; it's that "fight or flight" feeling. In the past, I experienced anxiety attacks to the point of hospitalization because I felt like I was having a heart attack. I can recall one incident where I was under so much stress in the workplace, the anxiety raised my blood pressure. My heart was racing, and I experienced neck and shoulders pain. It really felt like I was having a heart attack.

I'm not afraid to confess that not long ago I experienced anxiety attacks to the point that at times I'd wake up from a deep sleep in a panic. As I got closer to publishing this book, there was a period of time when I was experiencing these attacks almost nightly. I was getting little to no sleep and had to work the next day. Then one day during my quiet time with God, the Holy Spirit showed me the anxiety was an attack from the enemy to deter me from this mission. I sent out a text message to all the women whom I consider my prayer partners, asking them to agree with me in prayer for the attacks to stop.

Many replied expressing their prayerful support, and then one lady texted me, "Do you mind if I call you in thirty minutes to pray with you?"

"Not at all! I'll be waiting," I responded.

When she called me, she asked me what I was experiencing, and I shared what the Holy Spirit revealed to me—that the enemy was trying to deter me from publishing this book's message. She said, "If you're in your bedroom now, put me on speaker phone and let's pray."

That night we prayed against all anxiety attacks, both while I was awake and during my sleep. And then she prayed that God would reveal to me anything in the room that I needed to get rid of that may be invoking spiritual attacks.

After we prayed and ended the call, something came to my attention that I hadn't noticed before. It was a gift from a former friend that I kept because it was pretty. But as I looked at it, I realized why the object got my attention: it represented a past soul tie. I removed the object from my room and threw it out. That night—and every night since—I've had peaceful rest. (Well, except for when I'm having menopausal hot flashes!)

Yes, there are many ways to lower anxiety: mindfulness, physical exercise, breathing exercises, or talking with a friend or professional counselor. But honestly, there's no greater deterrent for anxious thoughts than trusting God.

Why? Because for believers, anxiety is rooted in doubt—that is, not trusting God to see you through whatever the situation may be. In the middle of the word *anxiety* is the letter *I*. The way you bulletproof your mind from anxiety is by stop trying to control every situation and trust God to be in control. Retraining yourself not to make the situation about you and learning to put it in God's hands is key in overcoming anxiety.

The Bible says, "Cast all your anxiety on him because he cares for you" (1 Pet. 5:7). And it tells us that "anxiety weighs down the heart, but a kind word cheers it up" (Prov. 12:25).

God not only wants us to know Him; He also wants us to believe Him! Many variables in our lives affect our willingness to trust God. A loss or betrayal can deeply mark our level of trust.

Depending on an unseen God doesn't come naturally to Christians with trust issues. Even those who don't have trust issues must learn to grow in their faith. A trust relationship grows only by stepping out in faith and making the choice to fully rely on God.

John 16:33 says:

> I have told you these things, so that in me you may have peace. In this

world you will have trouble. But take heart! I have overcome the world.

Let's break this verse down a bit. Notice the "sandwich" aspect of the message: You will have trouble here on earth, but take heart because I've overcome the world. This verse says you *will* have trouble, not that you *might*. That means troubles will always come.

Then God lowers the boom with the word *but*. But is a conjunction used to introduce a word or phrase that is going to contrast what has already been said. Jesus said, "*But* take heart, because I have overcome the world." In this, He is telling us: "I've overcome your feelings of anxiety, your fears, and your pain. I took them all on the cross and nailed them there. So why are you taking them down and carrying them around?" Jesus died so we wouldn't have to be burdened with anxiety. He already paid the price.

> *Trust is the key that opens the door to an anxiety-shattering flood of peace and joy.*

Trust is the key that opens the door to an anxiety-shattering flood of peace and joy. Do you trust God? I'm not talking about superficial, lip-service trust but the kind of trust that allows you to release whatever you've put your confidence in instead of God.

When we truly put our trust in the Lord, we will understand there is power in the name of Jesus, pray in the name of Jesus, and otherwise take authority over our enemies in the name of Jesus. This is how we will win our battles with anxiety and anything else that seeks to attack us.

Forgiveness Is Liberating

When someone hurts us, it can be difficult to forgive, but unforgiveness is an extremely dangerous emotion the enemy will use to put us in deep bondage. The battle to forgive comes in all shapes and sizes—the childhood or innocence you lost, the promotion you felt was rightfully yours but that was given to someone else, or the happily-ever-after ending you wished you had. But forgiveness doesn't mean you say the person didn't wrong you. Forgiveness simply means to release someone from a debt. Usually, it's a debt the offender could not repay even if they wanted to.

Forgiveness is not a suggestion. Jesus said:

> For if you forgive other people when they sin against you, your heavenly Father will also forgive you.
> —Matthew 6:14

Did you notice the condition in that verse? If you forgive others, then your heavenly Father will forgive you. In other words, you need to do your part first.

Why do we struggle to forgive those who have wronged us? Often it's because we think we're punishing the other person by not releasing the offense. The truth is that when we refuse to forgive, we imprison only ourselves with bitterness and anger. Unforgiveness paralyzes us and keeps us from walking in the fullness of our purpose because it causes us to focus on what is now behind us rather than on what lies ahead. By continuously focusing on the offense committed against us, we lose sight of the big picture—that is, what God has called us to do on a greater scale. It's like driving down the highway and constantly looking in the rearview mirror rather than looking ahead through the front windshield. You can't see where you're headed if you're constantly focused on what is now behind you.

I've always told my children, "If someone hurts you or does you wrong, forgive them and move on. Forgiveness is not for them; *it's for you.* When you forgive, you're releasing yourself from being imprisoned by bitterness, and you don't allow the other person to have control over your emotions or rule your life."

God in His infinite wisdom commands us to forgive because He knows unforgiveness holds us captive. Unforgiveness and the bitterness that typically accompanies it harm us, not our offender. The Scriptures say bitterness defiles us and makes us captive to sin (Heb. 12:15). But we are not only affected spiritually; we are affected physically as well.

Research shows that when we practice forgiveness, it has a positive impact on our physical and emotional wellbeing. Forgiveness is associated with lower levels of chronic anxiety and depression.[4]

Paul exhorted the believers in Ephesus: "And 'don't sin by letting anger control you.' Don't let the sun go down while you are still angry, for anger gives a foothold to the devil" (Eph. 4:26–27, NLT). The Greek word for devil in this verse (*diabolos*) can also be translated "slanderer."[5] By allowing unforgiveness to take root in our hearts, we give the offender a level of continuous control. We relive the offense over and over again, and the offender has moved on to live his or her life. If unforgiveness is left unchecked, we bear its weight to the point that past experiences hinder us from enjoying the blessings of God in the present. Taken a step further, carrying that weight of unforgiveness into the future can impact our choices because unforgiveness clouds our judgement.

Forgiveness is not earned because of something the offender does or doesn't do. It is freely given, just as Christ freely forgave us. Forgiveness is unconditional and one-sided. It is required whether or not reconciliation ever occurs.

> *To forgive is to set a prisoner free and discover that the prisoner was you.*
> —Lewis B Smedes

Forgiving those who offended or hurt me was never hard for me. However, forgiving myself was something I struggled with for a long time. I've always been hard on myself. If I felt I had failed God, then I would punish myself by thinking I wasn't worthy to receive God's grace and would run from God instead of approaching Him. What a lie! None of us is ever "worthy" to receive God's grace for all the wrong we've done. I've heard it said that grace is receiving what we don't deserve; that means we can never be worthy of it, which is why His grace is a gift and is freely given to us.

And newsflash: I still fail Him and fall short of God's standards, but when I do that, I've learned to forgive myself because I know I'm human and imperfect. I can acknowledge what I've done wrong and go to Him in repentance, asking for His grace and to make me whole again.

Learn how to forgive yourself so you don't imprison your soul in fear and go through life weighed down with insecurity, low self-esteem, anger, jealousy, and so on. Give yourself a chance to grow in God and overcome those dangerous emotions.

So how do you forgive? There's no special formula, but from a practical sense, here are seven steps you can take.

1. **Make a decision to forgive.** As I shared earlier, forgiving the offender is not for that person; it's for you. It's to guard your soul so bitterness does not take root in your life. But ultimately, you have to decide to forgive.
2. **Be specific.** Make a list of everything you feel you lost as a result of the wrong you experienced. If you can create a visual of the perceived offenses, then that's a step in the right direction to keep any resentment and bitterness from weighing you down.
3. **Pray for God's help**. There is no greater resource than taking your

burdens to your heavenly Father and asking Him to help you walk in forgiveness. When you pray, ask Him to reveal to you if there is any action you need to take.

4. **Decide that the offender doesn't owe you anymore**. This is a big one and a good indicator that you're truly walking in forgiveness. When you get to a point where you realize that the offender owes you nothing, then you protect your soul from harboring any unforgiveness.

5. **Choose to walk in forgiveness on a daily basis**. Like any decision to change your life for the better and walk in righteousness, choosing to forgive is a daily exercise. We must learn from our experiences and choose to grow.

6. **Bless them.** Choose to bless those who hurt you (Luke 6:28).

7. **Let it all go**. This needs no further explanation!

Your past doesn't define your present. Your present is a pathway to your future. Redirect your course if you're in an unhealthy state of mind and negative feelings prevail. Choose to forgive. As long as you're alive, it's never too late to start fresh.

He Accepts You Just as You Are

We all want to be loved and accepted, yet that doesn't always happen. We live in a broken world full of broken relationships, and sadly, rejection and abandonment are common. This shouldn't be, but it is.

Spouses choose to leave or reject their mate. Parents choose to reject or abandon their children. Some parents make it impossible for a child to please them so the child never receives the parents' blessing. Bosses or coworkers choose to reject someone in their workplace. At school, kids are rejected or mistreated by their peers. Some people are even rejected or mistreated at church.

When rejection or abandonment takes place, it pierces our heart in a way we may have never felt before. It can be easy to allow an event of rejection or abandonment to permanently define us, because rejection can make us feel as though we are inferior, broken, unlovable, damaged. Please realize this isn't true. You are a treasure. God made you, and you have always been part of His plan. You are *not* inferior to anyone. God wants to make you whole again—you are valuable and loved!

If you have been rejected or abandoned, I highly encourage you to take a moment to pour your deepest heartaches out to God. The Bible says, "The Lord is close to the brokenhearted; he rescues those whose spirits are crushed" (Ps. 34:18, NLT). Don't be afraid to draw close to God and share your heart. Allow Him to pour into your heart. Ask Him to reveal His plans and goals for your life.

There are many verses in Scripture about how much God loves those who have been rejected or abandoned. I believe this is because when people reject you, ultimately they're rejecting the One who created you. God will *never* leave you or abandon you (Deut. 31:6; Heb. 13:5), and His heart absolutely broke when someone chose to leave, abandon, mistreat, or reject you in the past.

You are in God's great heart. He is a safe haven you can trust. He loves and adores you! People who have been deeply hurt have an incredible ability to unconditionally love others. They have a compassion that is stronger than most.

> *People who have been deeply hurt have an incredible ability to unconditionally love others.*

Build your identity not on what others think about you but on what God says about you. The words of the psalmist paint a picture of just how deeply God loves you!

> I can never escape from your Spirit! I can never get away from your presence! If I go up to heaven, you are there; if I go down to the grave, you are there. If I ride the wings of the morning, if I dwell by the farthest oceans, even there your hand will guide me, and your strength will support me. I could ask the darkness to hide me and the light around me to become night—but even in darkness I cannot hide from you. To you the night shines as bright as day. Darkness and light are the same to you.
> —Psalm 139:7–12, NLT

God can take your life experiences and hurts and make them into something of great value for His kingdom. Ask God to heal your heart. Ask Him to work in your life, reveal His plans for you, and make His love come alive in you.

You have great worth, great value, and a great purpose. Please never doubt that.

What God Wants Us to Hear the Most

You aren't the mistakes you've made. You aren't the labels that have been put on you. And you aren't the lies the enemy has tried to sell you. *You are who God says you are.*

You are:

- a child of God (1 John 3:1)
- the apple of God's eye (Ps. 17:8)
- more than a conqueror (Rom. 8:37)
- a new creation in Christ (2 Cor. 5:17)
- the righteousness of Christ (2 Cor. 5:21)

All of our identity issues are fundamental misunderstandings of who God is. Guilt issues are a misunderstanding of God's grace. Control issues are a misunderstanding of God's sovereignty. Anger issues are a misunderstanding of God's mercy. Pride issues are a misunderstanding of God's greatness. Trust issues are a misunderstanding of God's goodness.

If you struggle with any of those issues, it's time to let God be the loudest voice in your life! God doesn't love you because of who you are. He loves you because of *who He is*.

When we succeed, God says, "I love you."
When we fail, God says, "I love you."
When we have faith, God says, "I love you."

When we doubt, God says, "I love you."

There is nothing you can do to make Him love you any more or any less. God loves you perfectly. He loves you eternally.

God wants us to hear what He's saying, and we must heed His voice. But more than that, He wants us to hear His heart. So He whispers more and more softly so we have to get closer and closer to hear. And when we finally get close enough, He envelops us in His arms and tells us that He loves us.

For too many of us, God's voice has been deafened by the voice of conformity, criticism, and condemnation, and the side effects include loneliness, shame, and anxiety. But there is good news.

You are not only made in God's image but you know His voice (John 10:4). He knit you together in your mother's womb (Ps. 139:13–14). He ordained all your days before one of them came to be (Ps. 139:16). The Bible says, "Being confident of this, that he who began a good work in you will carry it on to completion until the day of Christ Jesus" (Phil. 1:6). If you have trouble separating the truth found in God's Word from the lies you are bombarded with daily, consider spending more time in His Word on a regular basis. Remember: put on your belt of truth (see chapter 2).

Where is God leading you? How is He talking to you? If you can't hear His voice, consider spending more time in His Word on a regular basis.

Become the highest and best expression of who you were created to be. Don't try to become who someone else wants you to be. You were created with a God-designed purpose.

Your destiny is never in your shelter. Wonder Woman tried to hide on the island where her people lived to be sheltered from the real world, but her destiny would have never been fulfilled there. Likewise, you can't continue to hide on your own little island. You need to come out of your shelter, out of your hiding place, and discover the person God has called you to be.

Information Warfare Plan

Our hearts can deceive us if we allow our emotions to rule. This week think about "matters of the heart" and how God has armed you to protect it.

Recommended Daily Scriptures:
- Day 1: Proverbs 4:23
- Day 2: Romans 6:18; 15:13
- Day 3: 2 Corinthians 10:4-5
- Day 4: Ephesians 4:23-24
- Day 5: Hebrews 4:12–13
- Day 6: 1 Samuel 16:6–7
- Day 7: Isaiah 61:3

*Stand your ground....For shoes,
put on the peace that comes
from the Good News so that
you will be fully prepared.*
—Ephesians 6:14–15, NLT

Chapter 4

Boots on the Ground

No soldier should ever enter enemy territory without wearing combat boots. Prepared soldiers learn the enemy's tactics, and their feet are firmly planted so they can stand their ground when the enemy attacks. A soldier's boots need to have specific properties such as durability, water resistance, shock attenuation, ankle support, flexibility, and so on. In other words, the boots need to be durable enough to allow the soldier to hit the ground running.

My superhero, Wonder Woman, wears really cool boots, but it isn't the boots that endow her with super speed and enable her to leap high. It's her supernatural speed that propels her forward to do battle. But even she is not invincible. In one comic, when the villain Scarecrow released his fear gas, it caused her to give in to her deepest fears.[1]

We are constantly under attack, and we have a weapon that places us on the defensive. We defend ourselves by assuming a "ready stance" to stand firmly on God's Word and understand His grace without abusing it. We should be ready to share His Word with others and tell them how it has worked in our lives.

Being a Christian doesn't give us the right to walk all over others or allow people to use us as doormats. We should, however, be ready at all times to take the "gospel of peace" to all mankind, whether in word or deed, and do it lightning fast. Don't second-guess—if you see an opportunity, take it!

Regain Your Footing to Overcome

Just as physical battles always lead to casualties, so it is on the spiritual battlefield. Experiencing loss of any kind can leave you feeling unbalanced, hurt, hopeless, anxious, angry, faithless, and frustrated. And these feelings can cause you to lose your footing in the battle against the enemy.

In the midst of life's storms, I've lost my footing more times than I care to name. And in recent years I've learned more about death and dying than I ever cared to know. But what I'm about to share with you is not for pity's sake; it's to give you hope that you, too, can be restored.

I want to share with you my journey through the pain of divorce. If you have gone through divorce, then you understand it's one of the greatest losses you can experience in your lifetime. Divorce is like experiencing death but without a body to mourn. Even under what may appear to be the most civil circumstances, divorce is extremely painful. It is not only the couple who experiences the loss; the impact reverberates to extended family, mutual friends, and worst of all, the children from that marriage.

During and after my divorce, a couple of friends I had known most of my life turned their backs on me. Ironically, the friends who walked with me during that time were *not* Christians. The church I was attending at the time wasn't the spiritually healthy ministry I once believed it to be. I'm not blaming the church or friends—or anyone—for what I experienced during my divorce. No one is to shoulder the blame for my marriage falling apart except for my former spouse and me. We were accountable for (1) our individual relationships with God and (2) working together on the health of our marriage.

After a brief separation, I took my husband back for a period because I truly wanted to work things out and save our marriage. After all, I loved him. I had someone very close to me who found out that I had taken him back, and that person told me I was a "disappointment" and "weak." Those words were painful and wrong, and I ignored them because I truly wanted to try to work things out.

Throughout this time, I struggled to understand why our marriage was suffering. I don't know anyone who meets and marries another Christian and expects to later divorce. When I dwelled on all the events that transpired, the things said and done throughout our marriage and during the divorce, what the Lord highlighted for me was the area of my thought life. I had a lot to learn about the power of thoughts and how transformational they can be. Proverbs 23:7 says, "As [a man] thinks in his heart, so is he" (NKJV).

It took years of prayer, counseling, and acknowledging my own shortcomings to come to the point where God healed my mind and soul. Sadly, there are many people who can understand the pain I'm attempting to describe. But I also want you to know that you don't have to walk in shame because you're a divorced Christian. While God may have wanted to protect you from experiencing the pain, He is always going to love you just as you are. You can be restored to wholeness and live the life that God intended for you.

Today I'm grateful for the people who I know love me and have my back. I love them too and have their backs as well. That's what it means to have a "village."

Within three years after the divorce, I lost six loved ones. The loss of my marriage and so many loved ones was too much too bear. I felt like my mind and body never had a chance to recover from the previous loss before I was facing a new one.

> *While God may have wanted to protect you from experiencing the pain, He is always going to love you just as you are.*

But I've learned that when you're grieving, that's not the time to search for answers. Surviving the grieving process saps enough energy as it is, and the truth is, there are no answers that can adequately satisfy your longing to know, "Why, God?"

Eventually God helped me realize that life is way too short to sweat the small stuff. I learned to enjoy the good moments as they come and make positive memories. I learned to "eat dessert before dinner and take the trip," instead of putting things off for another time. I learned that appreciating the loved ones who are still with me and spending time with them are more important than slaving away at a job where I can easily be replaced. When I chose to change my perspective, God gave me beauty for ashes and turned my mourning into joy, as the prophet Isaiah declared.

> The Spirit of the Sovereign Lord is upon me, for the Lord has anointed me to bring good news to the poor. He has sent me to comfort the brokenhearted...To all who mourn in Israel, he will give a crown of beauty for ashes, a joyous blessing instead of mourning, festive praise instead of despair. In their righteousness, they will be like great oaks that the Lord has planted for his own glory.
>
> —Isaiah 61:1, 3, NLT

God is an incredible source of comfort, help, and love for the wounded soul. He knows all, He can heal all, and He has the ability to change any situation.

Seeing the proverbial "silver lining" during a time of loss, or gaining a new perspective, can be very challenging. But what I've learned during painful seasons in my life is that loss helps you to clearly see the good that remains in your life. It also allows you to learn from past mistakes or the error of other people's ways. It gives you a powerful opportunity to develop a deep gratitude for God and others.

The psalmist said, "He heals the brokenhearted and binds up their wounds" (Ps. 147:3). God is closer than you think when you're brokenhearted. Ask God to help you to create a "new normal" and be grateful for all the good He has given you in life every day.

> *There is purpose in your pain. You see the problem, but what you don't see is the purpose. The purpose is the* why, *and the problem is the* what.
> —TD Jakes

We all have different journeys we take in life, through bad times and good, but one thing is sure—if the Lord Jesus Christ is with us on the journey, we will make it through.

God gave me one life to live. I'm going to live it and make it count.

The Greater the Battle, the Greater the Victory

My grandmother Julia always said: "The greater the battle, the greater the victory." Wise words from a wise, godly woman. As I shared earlier, the battlefield of the mind is one in which we can gain victory by standing on what the Word of God says. Understanding the power of our thoughts isn't complicated. As a person thinks on the inside so will he or she become on the outside. Our character becomes the complete sum of our thoughts. As a plant springs from and could not exist without the seed, so does everything we do spring from the hidden seeds of our thoughts.

Thoughts grow not only into actions but also emotions. In fact, emotional turmoil could indicate that your predominant way of thinking is unhealthy and negative, and that harmful thoughts are influencing your life. The soul attracts what it desires, the things it loves, and that which it fears.

We think our thoughts can be tucked away in the recesses of our mind, but they can't. We believe, "These are just thoughts. How can they affect my life?" Our thoughts give birth to the habitual patterns of our lives. I encourage you to do as Paul encourages us in Philippians 4:8 and "fix your thoughts on what is true, and honorable, and right, and pure, and lovely, and admirable. Think about things that are excellent and worthy of praise" (NLT). Decide today to live free from negative and harmful thoughts and replace them with Godly thoughts.

Sometimes we make ourselves physically sick by worrying about things. And most of the time, it's a situation we have no control over. For example, you may really enjoy the work you do and the majority of your colleagues, but maybe the company has a toxic work environment. As a result, you're constantly bombarded with negative thoughts about not doing a good job or being let go. These are all *lies* from the father of lies, because if God gave you the job in the first place, then He will move you on in His time.

Remember, God has not abandoned or forsaken you. Regardless of your skills or who you know, you landed that job because God wanted you there. Your skills may have helped you gain a foot in the door, but they were not the driving force. You have been placed in that position purposefully. Examine why God may have you in that position. When the time is right, God will lead you into the next thing He has for you. Where He leads, He will provide. *Always.*

> *There is a purpose for everything you're going through in your life. But the revelation comes in retrospect; you'll look back and then receive revelation.*
> *— TD Jakes*

As a believer, I can pray about my situation and ask God for direction, and He will guide me. No matter how much a person speaks negatively to me or about me, I can overcome negativity by knowing I am who my Daddy says I am in Him. He has my back, and He will straighten out anyone who tries to rise up against me.

Our church has a discipleship program called Foundations, which culminates in a Victory Day, where leaders from the church pray with the participants. I've been in church all my life, and participating in Victory Day was one of the sweetest times of my life as a Christian. It renewed my life and my hope in God, and caused me to view life differently from that point on.

It was a day that also shifted my thought life and helped me to view life through God's lens instead of my distorted view. I began looking at all the blessings God had already given me—a beautiful home I never imagined I would have, a job that helped pay all my bills and allowed me to contribute to worthy causes, two healthy children, and a network of biological and spiritual family who demonstrate unconditional love.

Rather than looking at what you don't have or what has gone wrong, take time out each day to meditate on all that is beautiful and going well in your life. Stop allowing the enemy to bombard your mind with "stinking thinking." Such thinking only sabotages your present and your future.

What's in your soul—the seat of your emotions—attracts the same to you. You can overcome this through the power of the written Word and knowing what God says about you and who you are to Him. To remind yourself of this:

1. Put sticky notes with key verses and words of affirmation before your eyes each time you feel an attack coming. For example, if you're feeling inferior to someone, remind yourself that the Bible says God's children are "the head and not the tail" (Deut. 28:13).
2. Pray. Prayer is an intimate moment to openly communicate with Someone who deeply loves you and desires to be close to you. Don't put a time limit on prayer, but rather take time to hear what God speaks to your heart. You will know it's Him because you'll sense an overwhelming peace about what He's speaking to you.
3. Cut ties with anyone who subtracts from your life. Build relationships with people who add to your life—those who lift you up when you're down.

You are blessed and highly favored of God. Know that the bigger the battle, the bigger your victory will be. Maintain a "steady stance" in the midst of the battle and prepare to move forward.

Get on Your Feet!

How often have you heard that line, "Pull yourself up by your bootstraps and keep walking"? Those who work in the corporate world (or have worked in the corporate world) know full well it's a jungle out there, and only the strongest survive. Yes, if we'd recognize God as our boss, we'd realize that the things that stress us out in the workplace pale in comparison to Him, and in due time He will exalt us.

So if you're struggling on the job, first recognize that God is your boss. Then give your employers the respect they are due as the Bible instructs:

> Slaves, obey your earthly masters with respect and fear, and with sincerity of heart, just as you would obey Christ. Obey them not only to win their favor when their eye is on you, but as slaves of Christ, doing the will of God from your heart. Serve wholeheartedly, as if you were serving the Lord, not people, because you know that the Lord will reward each one for whatever good they do, whether they are slave or free.
> —Ephesians 6:5–8

Nothing is tougher than "obeying" a really lousy

boss. There are some people who simply shouldn't be managing others. The problem is when you don't have other job options and need a source of income.

I recall being in a position where the department head hated me so much that if looks could kill, I would've been dead. I don't know why the manager felt that way, as I did my best work and would go above and beyond when assigned a task or asked to do something. Eventually, a position opened up in the department that would have been a promotion for me. Although it meant directly reporting to the manager who vehemently hated me, I was willing to take on the challenge for the sake of doing what I enjoyed and getting a bump in my salary.

Then along came a contract worker who talked a good game but didn't produce. This smooth-talking contractor immediately impressed the manager. Six months later, the contractor got the job I had applied for—even though I was clearly more qualified and had more institutional knowledge. Adding insult to injury, I would now report to the contractor and would have to train the person to do the job. The culmination of that insult was when the manager who despised me trumped up a slanderous annual review to build a case to fire me.

The day the manager gave me the review, I was completely blindsided as the person cited incidents that had never transpired and times when I didn't show up for personal department events before or after work hours, claiming I wasn't a team player because I did not attend. I was warned that I was on a ninety-day probation. I felt like someone had punched me in the gut and knocked the wind out of me.

> *It's the Holy Spirit's job to convict. It's my job to love.*

I left work that day hysterical and cried all the way home. What would I do if I got fired? I needed to support myself and my two children. My salary was our only means of income.

When I got home, I was so shaken, even my kids didn't know how to react. I panicked. I remember calling a friend who is a human resources consultant and explaining the situation. Her advice to me was, "You better start polishing your resume because you're almost out the door."

That night I went to the women's small group at church and asked them to support me in prayer about my workplace situation. Over the next couple of months, I continued to train the contractor I was reporting to, do my job—and pray continuously.

During that time, God began to change my heart and the way I viewed the workplace. Driving home from work one day, I recall hearing in my heart, "Go to the store and buy a card congratulating [the former contractor] on the promotion." I thought, "Did I just hear You, God? It had to be You because there's no way in my flesh I'm going to say congratulations, much less buy her a card congratulating her for getting the job I should've had!" I had a full-blown, one-sided argument with God all the way to the store. I could just picture God looking at me, shaking His head as if to say, "Oh, Lillian, I love you!" Off I went to the store—and bought the card.

Another secret to success in the workplace is, "Humble yourselves, therefore, under God's mighty hand, that he may lift you up in due time" (1 Pet 5:6)! The more you humble yourself, both before God and man, the higher He will lift you up in His time! But you say, "Sure, I can humble myself before God, but how can I humble myself before my boss or coworker who insults me?"

Our job is to put others first and not worry about "our seat at the table." When we have this attitude, in due time God will cause our corporate colleagues to start to follow us, even if they don't officially report to us, because they will soon see that we have their best interest in mind. We will become leaders even without the official title, and eventually promotion will come.

What happened with the card and the former contractor? The next day before I went into the office, I prayed over the card. When the former contractor arrived at work that day, I walked over to her desk and handed her the card.

"It's for you, to congratulate you on getting the position," I said.

Her eyes opened wide, and she looked at me absolutely stunned. "Thank you," she said sheepishly.

I stood there as she read it. When she finished, she was so touched by the words of kindness in the card she was almost in tears. I asked her if I could give her a congratulatory hug, and she agreed. At that moment, I felt something instantly break in the atmosphere. Whatever negative feelings were in the air were gone. From that day on, we became good friends, and eventually she defended me before the manager who tried to fire me!

I had gained an ally and a friend. Even greater was my biggest defender—God—who didn't allow anyone to take me out of the job until He was ready. The other plot twist to this story was that I also had the support of the CEO when he found out what had transpired. He, too, came to my defense. When my time at the company ended, I left of my volition to a better position at another organization.

So be encouraged today. Keep doing the best you can, in sincere humility, knowing that God is the only source of your promotion. In due season, you will be promoted beyond your wildest dreams.

> *Don't allow what you do to define who you are.*

Allow whatever situation you are in to refine you, not define you.

Lean on Him

We need to bring our thoughts captive to the obedience of Christ and work on not dwelling on negative thoughts. In 2 Corinthians 10:5, Paul encourages the people of Corinth to "demolish arguments and every pretension that sets itself up against the knowledge of God, and...*take captive every thought to make it obedient to Christ*" (emphasis added).

Some people read this verse and think they should stop taking medication for anxiety or depression and instead take captive their thoughts. I'm not advocating for that. *Please do not discontinue any medication without the advice of your physician.* I do, however, believe that oftentimes mental illnesses thrive because we focus on our circumstances or what we see rather than exercising faith to believe what we do not see.

That's a lot easier said than done when a person battles depression or anxiety, but the turmoil can improve if you give your anxieties to God daily, maybe even as you experience them throughout the day. When you sense the fear, worry, or depression coming on, pause and pray. That's one way to overcome these challenges on a small scale.

Yes, leaning on God is the only way to get through a hostile work environment. As it says in Psalm 37:6, "He will make your righteous reward shine like the dawn, your vindication like the noonday sun." This is never easy because you want to retaliate and defend yourself, but you have to get out of the way and let God fight for you.

Remember what I went through and how that manager tried to get me fired? In the end, the executive of the company came to my defense, and I left in God's time for something better. Only God could orchestrate an exit strategy like that.

Whether you've experienced a broken relationship with family or friends or had loved ones pass away, you've probably rehearsed the "if I had only..." regrets. There are many things in life we can wish we had done differently, but please don't allow your regrets to define you. You are not a failure, a reject, or a loser. You're simply a human being who either made a poor decision or are living with the consequences of another person's unfortunate actions or decisions. Rather than allowing fear to paralyze you, allow the situation to catapult you into moving in faith.

From Fear to Faith

Fear is a very powerful emotion. Sometimes life dishes us situations over which we have little to no control. Not knowing what lies ahead can be scary, leaving us feeling exposed and helpless and wondering, *What will happen to me? How can I do this alone?* Satan's most destructive tool is fear. It causes people to cower into the corner and suffocates all rationality. It muddies the waters in our relationship with God, because it causes us to forget God's faithfulness in the past.

Physical challenges are difficult enough, but the emotional waves that roll over us can feel like the final blow. Yet God again provides a way of escape. Psalm 34:4 says, "I sought the Lord, and he answered me; he delivered me from all my fears."

When we feed our fears, we can fall into a frenzy. When we feed our faith, we fall into the comforting embrace of a loving Father. God settles threatening emotions.

God didn't give us a spirit of fear, but of love, power, and a sound mind that we may withstand temptation. (See 2 Timothy 1:7.) Even in the darkest circumstance we face, our greatest weapon against fear is the peace of God. Jesus said:

> I am leaving you with a gift—peace of mind and heart. And the peace I give is a gift the world cannot give. So don't be troubled or afraid.
> —John 14:27, NLT

Depending upon which Bible translation you're referencing, the word *peace* appears anywhere from 200 to 465 times in the Bible. In the New Living Translation, the word appears 362 times. That's a verse for almost every day of the calendar year. In other words, you don't have to go one day without the peace of God in your life. The enemy wants you to operate in fear, but God calls you to operate in faith.

The enemy wants you to operate in fear, but God calls you to operate in faith.

It's human nature to fear what's beyond our control. We were not created to always be in control, because if we were, we'd mess things up all the time! God asks us to relinquish control to Him, not to lord over us as a taskmaster but because He wants only His best for His daughters!

At each stage of life, we have different responsibilities and priorities. Currently, as a single working mom, I have different priorities and responsibilities than my married friends and my single friends without children.

Regardless of our current season in life—caring for elderly parents, raising children, building a career—we can know that it serves as preparation for a greater plan. Each person is made in God's image; we are all incredibly special, loved, and valuable.

God has a purpose and plan for your life that only *you* can accomplish. Now that's the truth!

Information Warfare Plan

What has been keeping you from experiencing peace in your life lately? Meditate on this week's scriptures and audibly declare that peace reigns over you.

Recommended Daily Scriptures:

- Day 1: John 14:26–27
- Day 2: Isaiah 26:3
- Day 3: John 16:33
- Day 4: Philippians 4:6–7
- Day 5: 1 Corinthians 14:33
- Day 6: Isaiah 53:5
- Day 7: Psalm 122

In addition to all this, take up the shield of faith, with which you can extinguish all the flaming arrows of the evil one.

—Ephesians 6:16

Chapter 5

Take Up Your Shield

Another weapon in Wonder Woman's arsenal is her shield, which is capable of deflecting any and all artillery fired directly at her. One of my favorite scenes in the 2017 *Wonder Woman* movie is when Diana ignores all the naysaying men, reveals her armor, climbs up a ladder, and rushes into battle in No Man's Land. Wow! As the German soldiers pellet her with their ammunition, she uses her shield to stand her ground, taking every hit to help the Allied soldiers. Then she advances, charging ahead to help the villagers caught behind enemy lines.

In combat, a shield is an offensive and a defensive weapon meant to protect against attacks and to safeguard a warrior as she charges into the heat of battle. Ephesians 6:16 says, "In addition to all this, take up the shield of faith, with which you can extinguish all the flaming arrows of the evil one." That phrase "in addition" means Paul was letting the believers in

Ephesus know their faith was part of their weaponry, and that other pieces were needed to complement their faith.

Faith is absolutely essential if we're to stand firm against temptation, or "the fiery arrows of the devil." While the breastplate of righteousness protects our vital organs, especially our heart (the soul), the shield of faith is meant to deflect negative thoughts, negative words (whether spoken directly to us or behind our backs), and temptations that hit us straight on or that come out of left field.

As believers, faith is foundational to our walk with God. Why? Because "without faith, it is impossible to please God, because anyone who comes to him must believe that he exists and that he rewards those who earnestly seek him" (Heb. 11:6).

Our faith is the buffer against all attacks on our body, mind, and soul. Using the shield of faith, we extinguish the temptations that come our way. Our shield of faith is intended to intercept very specific spiritual attacks and actively block attacks while we close in on the enemy in combat. The Bible says:

> My shield is God Most High, who saves the upright in heart. God is a righteous judge, a God who displays his wrath every day. If he does not relent, he will sharpen his sword; he

> will bend and string his bow. He has prepared his deadly weapons; he makes ready his flaming arrows.
> —Psalm 7:10–13

When it comes to the shield of faith, its purpose is to extinguish the "flaming arrows"—thoughts and actions—that give way to fear and doubt. Fear and doubt are the antithesis of faith. Faith is believing what we cannot see. It's trusting what we cannot see in the natural. It's walking in obedience even when what God has spoken doesn't make sense. You don't have to fully understand what God wants you to obey immediately. God's plan is often vague, not because He likes to toy with us but probably because if we saw the whole picture, we would run the other way! God leads us with one word: trust. Trust is an outcome of faith that God wants what's best for us.

> *The beautiful thing about this adventure called faith is that we can count on Him never to lead us astray.*
> —Chuck Swindoll

Stepping toward your destiny means stepping away from security. That is faith in action.

Press Past the Pain

Being in a constant battle for a period of time can wear you down emotionally and spiritually. Spiritual strength begins to wane, and inevitably you begin to lose faith and hope. Yet Proverbs 31:25 says, "Strength and honour are her clothing; and she shall rejoice in time to come" (KJV). You may not be rejoicing right now, but you shall rejoice in time to come. God has the ability to rebuild your hope, strength, and faith, and He is faithful to teach you new ways to fully trust in Him. He frequently reminds those going through loss to "be still, and know that I am God!" (Ps. 46:10, NLT). That is easier said than done, but to those who trust God, great things will come out of their times of loss.

It never does anybody any good to remain stagnant in an ocean of what-ifs, if-onlys, or negative emotions. We must train ourselves to take our heartaches, questions, and negative emotions to God and allow Him to use them as fuel to help us instead of harm us.

Pressing forward can be super difficult, but if we allow God to work in our hearts and through our circumstances, He receives glory for the outcome, whether it is great or small. God can use any situation, regardless of its size, to bless your life and the lives of others. Ask God to help you develop the courage and faith you need to press forward past the pain.

Ask Him to help you to make the changes you need in your heart and attitude to please Him. There will be days when you feel weak. In those days, realize that in your weakness, He is strong, and He will carry you through (2 Cor. 12:9–10). When you love God and your ways are pleasing to Him, He is faithful to make your path straight.

Ridiculous Faith

Sometimes our situations call for ridiculous faith. What do I mean by "ridiculous"? I suppose I could get technical and give you the definition of the word *ridiculous,* but that's not where I'm headed here. I'm talking about having the kind of faith that is willing to step out of the boat and onto the water, as Peter did in Matthew 14:22–33.

Think about something you've been praying for. Why hasn't the answer to that prayer materialized yet? The answer is something that only God knows. Maybe the answer hasn't manifested yet because what you have in mind and what God wants to accomplish through you are two different things. The Lord said:

> "My thoughts are nothing like your thoughts…And my ways are far beyond anything you could imagine. For just as the heavens are higher

> than the earth, so my ways are higher than your ways and my thoughts higher than your thoughts."
>
> —Isaiah 55:8–9, NLT

His thoughts and ways are higher than your own. Trust Him to work above and beyond the limitations of your current level of faith. Faith that is put to work matters to God! He's looking for people who have faith and will trust Him to do what He promised. The problem, however, is that most of the time we put limitations on our faith.

Take Philip, for example. When Jesus asked Philip how they could feed the huge crowd that had gathered to hear Jesus speak, Philip saw limitations, but Jesus saw an opportunity for him to grow in faith.

> When Jesus looked up and saw a great crowd coming toward him, he said to Philip, "Where shall we buy bread for these people to eat?" He asked this only to test him, for he already had in mind what he was going to do.
>
> Philip answered him, "It would take more than half a year's wages to buy enough bread for each one to have a bite!"

> Another of his disciples, Andrew, Simon Peter's brother, spoke up, "Here is a boy with five small barley loaves and two small fish, but how far will they go among so many?"
>
> Jesus said, "Have the people sit down." There was plenty of grass in that place, and they sat down (about five thousand men were there). Jesus then took the loaves, gave thanks, and distributed to those who were seated as much as they wanted. He did the same with the fish.
>
> —John 6:5-11

Jesus was testing Philip's faith. Jesus already knew the miracle He was going to perform to multiply the boy's meal, but He wanted to stretch Philip's faith beyond the obvious physical limitations he saw. And Philip didn't pass the test; he had to do a makeup exam. Instead, another disciple, Andrew, saw an opportunity where Philip saw limitation.

Andrew not only saw an opportunity for Jesus to supply food for the crowd, but he also acted upon his faith. Andrew brought the boy to Jesus who had five loaves of bread and two small fish. In the natural, that wasn't much to feed about five thousand men (there were far more when you count the women and the children). But in God's hands even a Long John Silver Value Meal, as my pastor describes it, can stretch to supply everyone's needs.

> *Conquest without confronting the issues leads to false victory. You have to confront the issues in order to conquer those areas and experience true victory.*
> *—TD Jakes*

God says, "Show Me your faith, and I'll show you My faithfulness."

When God Seems Silent

Have you ever wondered why God sometimes doesn't answer us in times of great need? One reason may be because we willingly continue to sin and scoff at wisdom. God attempts to get our attention, but we rebelliously make the decision to keep going in the wrong direction.

We need to consider what God sternly warns us about in the first chapter of Proverbs. God cries out for us to listen to Wisdom.

> Wisdom shouts in the streets. She cries out in the public square. She

> calls to the crowds along the main street, to those gathered in front of the city gate: "How long, you simpletons, will you insist on being simpleminded? How long will you mockers relish your mocking? How long will you fools hate knowledge? Come and listen to my counsel. I'll share my heart with you and make you wise."
>
> —Proverbs 1:20–23, NLT

Anytime we go through a heartbreaking problem due to our poor choices, we have to admit that our pain is ultimately self-inflicted. Loss and grief that are self-inflicted usually happen because of continual and willful sin—when at some point we chose to turn our hearts away from God and fulfill our needs, wants, and desires apart from Him and His will.

Think about it. God gives each of us a heart that only He can truly satisfy, but instead of going to Him to meet our needs, we try to fill our heart with counterfeits. We were built to need genuine love and fellowship from God, yet so many of us seek to find that love and fellowship through ungodly relationships, distractions, and addictions.

The *only* one who can truly satisfy our soul is the One who created it.

> *Don't mistake delays for destiny. Just because you've been delayed does not mean you've been denied. Sometimes people forfeit their destiny because they can't endure the process. Endure the process so you can reach your destiny.*
> —T.D. Jakes

I've said it before but it bears repeating: If we are heading down the wrong road, we need to make a stunning, screeching stop, and turn around. We need to leave our sin, repent, start obeying God, and make a big U-turn to start following God's will for us.

Ask God to reveal to you the things in your life He does not approve of. What breaks His heart needs to break your heart, too.

You can do all things through Christ who gives you strength (Phil. 4:13). If there is sin in your life, God can empower you to break free of what binds you and start over.

Authentic Faith

I love chocolate diamonds. Perhaps because seeing

a diamond that color makes me think of one of my favorite sweets—chocolate. The truth is these precious stones are brown diamonds. It was the LeVian® company that trademarked the name Chocolate Diamond® to describe it in a way that made the stone seem more desirable and increase its value.[1] That was a clever marketing angle because the word *chocolate* often evokes thoughts of richness and luxury. The word *brown* when coupled with *diamond* evokes thoughts of something being dirty, low quality, and less valuable.

Brown diamonds are found mostly in places like Australia, Angola, Borneo, Brazil, and the Congo.[2] In fact, these diamonds can be just as beautiful and colorless as the common white diamonds. The fact the diamonds are brown doesn't diminish their authenticity. But the color of a diamond doesn't matter to its owner because it's still beautiful, flaws and all.

Like a brown diamond, we don't need to be flawless to be authentic about our faith. Our flaws actually validate us as authentic. In fact, if we represent ourselves as flawless, then we most certainly declare ourselves as fake.

You can present yourself to others as flawless and project an edited version of yourself to the world. In today's world of social media, people project an edited version of themselves frequently. There are apps to remove blemishes, wrinkles, even help shed a few pounds!

Nobody is perfect except for God—so let Him be the One to fill in the gaps in your life. Where you feel inadequate, He is more than able. Where you lack, He is more than enough. Where you may struggle to find your footing, His grace sufficient.

The apostle Paul states, "My grace is sufficient for you, for My power is made perfect in weakness" (1 Cor. 12:9, NIV). In that same verse, Paul goes on to say, "Therefore I will boast all the more gladly about my weaknesses, so that Christ's power may rest on me."

He is more than faithful to reveal Himself through your imperfections, so there is no need to hide them. Authentic faith doesn't seek to cover up all its imperfections and weaknesses. Rather, it understands that our imperfections are the very places God chooses to reveal Himself to and through us.

Stop hiding the real you from the world. Have the courage to be yourself, and be true to who God created you to be. In a world full of characters carefully crafting their image, drop the façade, trusting that the real value is not in others seeing you as perfect, but in others seeing God's grace revealed in your imperfections.

Press the Restart Button

Did you know there's a restart button on every person? I didn't know that until one day when I witnessed a husband and wife having, well, a "discussion."

The wife was babbling on, and I could see the husband's jaw tense with every word his wife spoke. She wouldn't come up for air, much less let him get a word in edgewise. Oblivious to her husband's irritation, the wife would jump from one subject to the next and in between ask her husband, "Honey, did you hear what I said? You'd better be listening to me!"

That poor man stared off into space as his wife continued her mindless chatter. Finally, when he'd had enough, the husband got up from his chair, walked over to his wife, and ever so gently placed his index finger in the middle of her forehead, pressed it, and went back to sit in his easy chair.

Stunned by this random act, the wife stopped talking. After a few seconds, she looked at him and gently said, "What was that for?" Maintaining his calm demeanor, he looked at her and said, "Dear, the conversation wasn't going anywhere, so I thought if I pressed your restart button, we could start over and both get a word in."

I died laughing.

Honestly, though, how many times do we get so caught up in ourselves that we forget to pause and listen to others or to what God is trying to say to us?

During one Sunday afternoon church service, I was serving in the media ministry. My pastor was teaching a series called "Re*Start." This Sunday happened to be week three in the series, and the sermon was titled "Re*New." He shared how the word *renew* comes from the Greek term *anakainoō*,[3] which means *to renovate* or *renew*.

Sharing from Colossians 3:10, he said we need to learn to put on our new nature, and our strength will be renewed. When we do this, we become like Jesus. We don't allow the situation to overtake us; instead, we become victorious. It's not about our own strength; it's about Him. It's about being steadfast, regardless of the situation.

David prayed, "Create in me a pure heart, O God, and renew a steadfast spirit within me" (Ps. 51:10). And we read in Isaiah 40:31 that "those who hope in the Lord will renew their strength. They will soar on wings like eagles; they will run and not grow weary, they will walk and not be faint."

When you get tired, remain steadfast in faith, rest in Him, and allow the Lord to renew your strength. Rest, queen.

Information Warfare Plan

When was the last time you invited the Holy Spirit to speak to you, and you actively listened? What was the result when you activated your faith?

Recommended Daily Scriptures:

- Day 1: Isaiah 40:29
- Day 2: Luke 5:17–20
- Day 3: Psalm 57:7
- Day 4: James 1:2–3
- Day 5: James 4:7
- Day 6: Hebrews 11
- Day 7: Joshua 10

Take the helmet of salvation...
—**Ephesians 6:17**

Chapter 6

Queen in Training

I used to love watching the *Wonder Woman* TV show and seeing Lynda Carter take the tiara off her head and fling it at the enemy—*whack!*—where it would then boomerang back to her. Wonder Woman's gold tiara doesn't necessarily weaken her, but it isn't there to protect her head, which leaves her somewhat vulnerable to potential harm.

While in the process of writing this book, I had the opportunity to visit Greece—a beautiful country filled with lovely people, rich culture, and so much history. During the visit to ancient Olympia, I was able to tour a museum that houses relics, including ancient weapons and armor. During that visit, I learned that the bronze "Corinthian" helmet was the most widely used helmet in the archaic and early classical periods. Over time, the Greeks adjusted the anatomical details of the helmet to make it better fit the warrior's head.

Like the ancient Greek warriors, we have a helmet as part of our armor—it's called the helmet of salvation. It serves to protect our "head"—primarily our relationship with God and secondarily our households. If the head is wounded in battle, then the rest of the body can't function. Similarly, if our most critical relationship is damaged, everything in our lives, including every other relationship, will be affected. We are queens in training, and as such we should guard and carefully manage our salvation and relationship with God.

Mi Reina

For my daughter's sweet sixteenth birthday, I surprised her with a piece of jewelry: a rose gold tiara ring with tiny crystals. Mind you, she had been eyeballing it for months before her birthday and kept dropping hints that she wanted it. She knew how to get me to eventually buy it for her. But the reason I bought it wasn't to indulge her wants; the ring was meant to symbolize that she is my little "queen in training."

How often do we refer to our daughters as our little princesses? But a princess does not always become a queen who inherits the kingdom. In Latin culture, it's not uncommon to hear a woman referred to as *mi reina (my queen)* because of the value placed upon her. I wanted my daughter to know she's in training—as all of God's daughters are—to someday inherit her Father's kingdom. She is a "queen in training," and her Father—the King of kings and Lord of lords—is molding her to someday inherit the kingdom He has promised her as a child of God. (See 1 Corinthians 6:9–11.)

God has made this promise to you, too, but do you believe it? How deep does your faith run? Do you realize your Father owns cattle on a thousand hills (Ps. 50:10), and all of it is yours to inherit? Jesus paid the price of our salvation, and it is our responsibility to work out our salvation "with fear and trembling" (Phil. 2:12). Don't twist the meaning here. It's not a matter of being afraid of God or anything along the path He invites us to walk through this life. This fear is a holy awe or reverence. Think about it. The Creator of the universe, the One who spoke the heavens into existence, came down to the earth in human form to die a death that we should have suffered so we can live and experience abundant life.

There is something about trusting God with your life that opens your mind's eye to a whole other dimension you wouldn't experience otherwise.

As believers, we can trust that He has called us to be different than the world. The way we live and think should be different, and part of wearing the helmet of salvation is to develop the mind of Christ (Phil. 2:5). Understand that the real power of transformation lies in understanding that taking on the mind of Christ to one day rule and reign with Him is our inheritance as children of God and, specifically, as queens in training.

This is the salvation that we do battle for—to inherit the kingdom as joint heirs with Christ.

> And if [we are His] children, [then we are His] heirs also: heirs of God and fellow heirs with Christ [sharing His spiritual blessing and inheritance], if indeed we share in His suffering so that we may also share in His glory.
>
> —Romans 8:17, AMP

And no matter what the enemy throws at us, no matter how intense the battles become, we have confidence in knowing that so long as we remain in Him, we will ultimately gain the victory.

That victory will result in someday being compensated with a crown.

> I have fought the good fight, I have finished the race, I have kept the faith. Finally, there is laid up for me the crown of righteousness, which the Lord, the righteous Judge, will

> give to me on that Day, and not to me only but also to all who have loved His appearing.
> —2 Timothy 4:7–8, NKJV

Each day we should live out our lives, knowing that each day we must make a choice to take on the mind of Christ in all we say and do. That doesn't mean there won't be times when we stumble. But when we do, we get back up and make a conscious decision to live for Him. It's an ongoing process, not a one-and-done event.

As part of our ongoing conversion, we meditate on God's Word so we can follow it (Heb. 10:16) and be transformed in our minds (Rom. 12:2). In so doing, we set aside a battle-axe mentality that things need to be done our way rather than God's way.

Get Rid of the Battle-Axe Mentality

Please stick with me in this section. Something that no amount of education, counseling, or discipleship can ever teach women is how to stop being a nag and tearing your man down. It's what I refer to as a "battle-axe mentality," the idea that if the men in your life don't do as you say or jump as high as you want, heads will roll!

How many times have you heard a man describe a woman as an old battle-axe? Where do you think that idiom came from? It correlates to Ephesians 6:17, because if a Roman soldier's helmet was missing or not on right and an enemy came with a battle-axe, heads would roll. Think of all the good men who have lost their heads in the heat of a battle with a domineering woman!

The term *old battle-axe* means "a bossy old woman."[1]

As I shared earlier, I grew up in a strong, matriarchal family—of Latinos, no less. If you know anything about Hispanic women, you know that if the man tells her, "*Aquí mando yo* (I'm in charge here)," she just looks at him and laughs. In my family, we have a running joke that all the women outlast their husbands. There is truth in jest. I had two aunts who each outlived two husbands!

We joke all the time about the strong personalities of the women in our family. But all joking aside, we as women need to lay down the battle-axe mentality and let our men be men.

The true origin of a battle-axe mentality is found in ancient times. When the Romans ruled over most of the civilized world, a Roman soldier was considered stupid if he went into battle without his helmet. It was the last piece of armor that a soldier would put on. An article I read recently said this about the helmet:

> A helmet protects a soldier against damaging and deadly blows to the head. Spiritually speaking, the helmet of salvation provides hope and protects the mind against anything that would disorient or destroy the Christian, such as discouragement or deceit.[2]

Bible teacher and missionary Rick Renner had this to say about the helmet of salvation:

> If your salvation is not worn tightly around your mind like a helmet, the enemy will come to chop the multiple blessings of your salvation right out of your theology. He will try to hack away at your foundation, telling you that healing, deliverance, preservation, and soundness of mind were not really a part of Jesus' redemptive work on the Cross. [The enemy] can try to manipulate your emotions, send signals of sickness and disease into your body, and so on. To protect you from such attacks is the very

reason God has given you the "helmet of salvation."³

Fitting yourself each day with the helmet of salvation protects you from attacks against your emotions and your mind. Then you can face your battles knowing the enemy can't easily knock your block off!

From the Clearance Rack to the Glass Case

As I shared with you in an earlier chapter, how others perceive you is not your reality, nor does their opinion about you matter. You are very valuable to God, and He loves you unconditionally. What you need to start realizing is your *self-worth*.

As women, we set the tone for how people treat us, especially when it comes to our relationships with men. Sometimes we have devalued our self-worth because of the emotional scars from past relationships. Those scars may have been the result of past sexual encounters when we weren't walking close to God, and with each encounter, a little piece of us was left behind. Eventually, we begin to feel unworthy when we should carry the truth within us that there is one Man who values us so much He longs to protect us from hurt. His name is Jesus.

> *No one can make you feel*
> *inferior without your consent.*
> *—Eleanor Roosevelt*

You are more precious than rubies (Prov. 31:10), but you must believe that. Quit putting yourself on the clearance rack for guys who don't deserve you and, worse yet, don't recognize your value! Move yourself from the clearance rack to the locked glass case where the valuables are kept.

Oftentimes as women we don't take the time to seek the help needed to receive healing from past hurts and failures. We're so focused on being caregivers and meeting the needs of others that we neglect our own well-being. As caregivers we don't want to become a burden to others, so we struggle with showing signs of vulnerability and acknowledging our need for help. There's much more awareness today that people struggle with mental health issues, and there is greater acceptance of seeking help from a professional counselor, therapist, or psychologist. Many employers include well-being plans as part of their benefits packages, and most churches today offer professional counseling, often at little to no cost. There are resources to tap into to get the help needed.

I can relate to the need for counseling. After experiencing so much loss—the loss of my marriage and the loss of loved ones through death—my life began to spiral out of control, and I fell into a deep depression. My self-worth was so low I didn't feel I deserved to have anything good in my life. This was the enemy, of course. God desires to bestow good things on those who love Him (Ps. 84:11). It was during this low point of my life that I began to seek God again and found a professional Christian counselor.

My counselor was a godsend, and she helped me overcome the depression by showing me how to reframe my thinking and set boundaries. She also gave me the tools to rediscover my self-worth. She always closed each counseling session by asking, "Can I pray with you?" I loved that! Prayer always brought me peace.

She helped me see life through a different lens and understand that setting boundaries for the sake of my well-being is not just acceptable; it's normal. I began to realize that if I wasn't healthy in every area of my life, then I couldn't care for anyone else. There was nothing wrong with loving myself.

Hear me loud and clear: there is *nothing* wrong with getting the help you need, and that extends beyond mental health counseling. If you are in a situation that is harming you in some way, seek help. Any kind of abuse—physical, emotional, sexual, financial, etc.—should never be tolerated—period. I've witnessed the mark that abuse leaves on a woman's life. Even long after the physical scars heal, the emotional and mental wounds often remain open if the victim doesn't receive the help needed.

Usually a tangible type of abuse heals faster than an intangible one such as emotional abuse. On top of that, those who have suffered abuse often don't seek the help needed to fully heal and be free from the pain of the past. What ends up happening quite often is that the pain is carried into the next relationship, and when that relationship doesn't work out, the past pain is compounded, and it becomes harder to develop healthy relationships.

An emotionally unhealthy woman operates from her pain instead of her purpose. She attempts, in vain, to build a relationship, and at the first sign of a perceived offense, she reacts and may even seclude herself as a self-defense mechanism.

I once read a powerful and incredibly true statement on Twitter. The blogger wrote: "An unhealed person can find offense in pretty much anything someone else does. A healed person understands that the actions of others has absolutely nothing to do with them. Each day you get to decide which one you'll be."[4]

> *An unhealed person can find offense in pretty much anything someone else does. A healed person understands that the actions of others has absolutely nothing to do with them. Each day you get to decide which one you'll be.*

Sadly, the unhealthy woman ends up pushing away the relationship she longs to experience. If she would only seek the help she needs to heal her emotions and recognize that God can completely heal her, then she will realize that how others act has nothing to do with her. How others act toward her has everything to do with their personal journey to wholeness.

The enemy knows your weaknesses, but do you?

Part of any strategic battle plan is knowing your enemy's tactics and moves—how he plans to come at you in order to tear you down. However, that doesn't mean the enemy will never trip you up and cause you to fall. It's not a matter of *if* you will fall but *when* you do. And God promised to see you through it all. The prophet Isaiah declared:

> When you go through deep waters, I will be with you. When you go through rivers of difficulty, you will

not drown. When you walk through the fire of oppression, you will not be burned up.

—Isaiah 43:2, NLT

No matter how overwhelmed you may feel, you will get through it. This too shall pass. It might feel like a kidney stone at the time, but it'll pass.

Straighten Your Crown and Dare to Be Y-O-U

There's a social media meme that shows a group of little girls all dressed as princesses, some in purple and some in blue—except for one little girl donning a Batman costume. The caption says: "In a world full of princesses, dare to be Batman." That girl in the Batman costume is so me! Don't ever tell me to do something, because I'll do the exact opposite. I'm not a follow-the-crowd kind of gal; I'm a follow-me type of person.

As a kid, I was always around my cousins. Back in the days before social media, video games, and the internet, we had to use something called *imagination,* and being social meant we had to actually interact with others (smile). Often two of my male cousins and I would role play as Batman, Robin, and Batgirl. One cousin was always Batman, the other was always

Robin, and that left me as Batgirl. That was really my only option because Catwoman was a villain, and I was not much of a cat lover. We'd run around the house singing the theme song to the sixties version of the Batman television show and fighting imaginary crime. In the end, good always won.

Role-playing keeps the mind active and young, but it's not meant to be part of our identity. Who we truly are is found in who God says we are: *beautiful and chosen* (1 Peter 2:9; John 15:16); *lovely, a priceless pearl, and precious in His sight* (Isa. 43:4). Whenever the enemy tells you otherwise, meditate on these scriptures and search for others that speak to you.

> *If you are always trying to be normal, you'll never know how amazing you can be.*
> —Maya Angelou

As women, we tend to lose our identity and true sense of self because we think that by morphing into whatever role the world around us says we need to play, we will be accepted. I say no! Don't accept the status quo or any mold this world tries to shoehorn you into. Stand firm in the knowledge that you are royalty and chosen to serve as a manager of all that God has entrusted to you.

The Bible says, "But you are a chosen people, a royal priesthood, a holy nation, God's special possession, that you may declare the praises of him who called you out of darkness into his wonderful light" (1 Pet. 2:9). The Greek word translated "possession" in that verse is *peripoiēsis,* meaning to preserve or make one's own property.[5]

Does that mean you're a slave to God, unable to make your own choices? No! It's not that kind of possession. It means you were so valuable to God that He willingly sacrificed everything to have you in His life. That's how much you mean to Him! Have you ever met any human being who would do that for you? I haven't. Everyone has limits to what they'll sacrifice for someone else.

> *Be who you were created to be, not what someone else thinks you should be.*

We're human; it's our nature to be self-preserving. But God is so perfect in all His ways that there's nothing we can do to make Him turn away from us or to love us any less. His love is unconditional and knows no bounds.

First Peter 2 goes on to say:

> Once you were not a people, but now you are the people of God; once you

> had not received mercy, but now you
> have received mercy.
> —1 Peter 2:10

These days, the only opinion I count on is God's, and I already know what it is. I'm His daughter; I'm a queen in training to someday inherit my Father's kingdom. Until then, I do all that He asks me to do—love Him, love people, and serve to influence the lives of those around me.

Yes, in world of fairytale princesses, dare to be different. Be who *you were created to be,* not what someone else thinks you should be. Stand tall and straighten your crown, queen in training.

Information Warfare Plan

As you read the daily scriptures and meditate on each one, take note of the ways the enemy may attack your spiritual identity. Think about how you can solidify your thinking to strengthen your relationship with God.

Recommended Daily Scriptures:

- Day 1: James 1:2-3, 12
- Day 2: James 1:21–22
- Day 3: Esther 2: 15-18
- Day 4: Esther 4:11-14
- Day 5: Ephesians 2:8
- Day 6: Philippians 2:12-13
- Day 7: Psalm 139:1–6, 13–17

*Take...the sword of the Spirit,
which is the word of God.*
—Ephesians 6:17

Chapter 7

The god-Killer

In another scene from the 2017 *Wonder Woman* film, Diana comes face-to-face with Ares, the Greek god of war. When he reveals his identity, she wields the god-killer sword at him, only to have it disintegrate in his hands. What she later discovers is that the god-killer wasn't the sword itself; it resided within her. She was the weapon.

> *Life is killing all the time*
> *and so the goddess kills*
> *herself in the sacrifice of her*
> *own animal.*[1]
> —Quote engraved on Wonder Woman's sword

The sword described in Ephesians 6—the sword of the Spirit, which is the Word of God—is an offensive weapon against the enemy. We use it to kill the "gods" in our lives not by flashing it to the enemy but by releasing its truth into the atmosphere.

The Bible says God's Word will accomplish that for which it was sent (Isa. 55:10–11). When we declare God's Word, we not only remind ourselves of who we are in Him, but we deal devastating blows to our enemy. Instead of continuing to advance against us, he will have to retreat when we choose to believe and speak God's Word over ourselves and our situation.

We'll take a look at two ways to activate the sword of the Spirit. First, we absorb the Scripture in our hearts and then declare it aloud when we're attacked. Second, we verbalize the Scriptures during our prayer time.

You Speak and God Breathes Life Into Your Circumstances

The Word of God is the most powerful weapon within your arsenal. It was there in the beginning of Creation:

> In the beginning, God created the heavens and the earth. Now the earth was formless and empty, darkness was over the surface of the deep, and the Spirit of God was hovering over the waters.
>
> And God *said*...
>
> —GENESIS 1:1–3 , EMPHASIS ADDED

God gave us an example of the power of the spoken Word. He didn't have to speak to create; He's an omnipotent God! Yet He spoke the Word, and life was created. Then thousands of years later, the Word came alive—personified in His Son, Jesus Christ.

> In the beginning was the Word of God and the word was with God, and word was God.
> —John 1:1, KJV

The Amplified Bible puts it this way:

> In the beginning [before all time] was the Word (Christ), and the Word was with God, and the Word was God Himself.

Jesus also knows the power of the spoken Word as a weapon. He *is* the Word of God Himself. Before He begins His ministry, we see Him fasting for forty days in the wilderness. (See Matthew 4:1–11.) During this time, Jesus was preparing internally. Before He ever taught others externally, He filled up on Scripture and prepared for opposition through prayer. If Jesus, being God, devoted Himself to knowing God's Word and spending time in prayer, then how much more should we?

When you spend time consistently with God through reading His Word and talking with Him through prayer, the Holy Spirit will be faithful to help you know when something doesn't honor God.

God's Word is a way to wage war on the enemy. God will help you know the difference in discerning His voice from all others as you continually seek Him.

I remember attending the Every Nation Ministry GO! Conference in the summer of 2019. Pastor Chris Johnson of Divine Unity Community Church in Harrisonburg, Virginia, spoke on Campus Night, and his message was based on Ezekiel 37:1–10, the account of the valley of the dry bones. What's so spectacular about this? Well, for one, it was a message God had repeatedly shared with me through a close friend and prayer partner, during my devotional time, in worship songs, and now through Pastor Chris.

In the story, God asked Ezekiel a question:

> And he said unto me, Son of man, can these bones live? And I answered, O Lord God, thou knowest.
>
> —Ezekiel 37:3, KJV

God asked the question not because He didn't already know the answer, but because He wanted faith to arise in Ezekiel that he could be part of God's plan.

> So I prophesied as I was commanded. And as I was prophesying, there was a noise, a rattling sound, and the

> bones came together, bone to bone. I looked, and tendons and flesh appeared on them and skin covered them, but there was no breath in them. Then he said to me, "Prophesy to the breath; prophesy, son of man, and say to it, 'This is what the Sovereign Lord says: Come, breath, from the four winds and breathe into these slain, that they may live.'" So I prophesied as he commanded me, and breath entered them; they came to life and stood up on their feet—a vast army.
>
> —Ezekiel 37:7–10

Ezekiel activated his faith, releasing the power of God's Word. Big faith is believing in something so much bigger than you that only God can accomplish it.

When God's power breathes on you, it enlivens the dream that dwells inside of you—that dream that's been lying dormant in your heart for a really long time because you've been afraid of stepping out and failing. As God told the prophet Isaiah, "Behold, I will do a new thing; now it shall spring forth; shall ye not know it? I will even make a way in the wilderness, and rivers in the desert" (Isa. 43:19, KJV).

Never was God's power to breathe life into dead bones more alive to me than when I was writing this book. For years, it has always been my heart's desire to become an author and write for a living. Writing and publishing are my passion! I *love* to write! During my journey, a sweet friend of mine sent me this text one day, and it awakened something in me:

> Interestingly enough Ezekiel had to prophesy over the bones to see this happen. I just read this chapter [Ezekiel 37] this morning. What if the Lord is trying to speak to you that He is breathing life into those areas that you once dreamed about that have gone dry? That He wants you to prophesy over your God-given dreams that He wants to bring life to now? Does this resonate with you?

It sure did resonate with me! I knew this prophetic word that my friend shared was God breathing life into a dream that I thought was dead. I had regained hope and encouragement to fulfill my dream as an author. There is another dream too, but that will come in His timing, not mine.

Despite the setbacks, detours, and pit stops you face, remember that God has a purpose for you that will be fulfilled.

> So is my word that goes out from my mouth: It will not return to me empty, but will accomplish what I desire and achieve the purpose for which I sent it.
>
> —Isaiah 55:11

God's Word is a reminder to you that He is timeless. He is not bound by time because He created time. Stand firm and know that no matter what you face, God's promise to activate wisdom in your life will come to pass. Don't think for one moment that God will not show up on time for you, even if everything in you is screaming it's hopeless and it appears to be too late. God has a plan for your life, and He will fulfill that plan in His time.

Even unbelievers know the power of the spoken word. How often do we hear people say, "Don't put that negativity into the atmosphere" or, "I'm sending good vibes your way." Oh, really? How is it unbelievers tend to have more faith in the power of the spoken word than believers who have experienced the power of the living God?

We have a great weapon—the Word of God that breathes new life. It overwhelms every kind of evil—spoken or otherwise—in our lives. If we commit to using the weapon of the Word, then we can wield it against our enemy and his cohorts. When we wield the sword of the Spirit by speaking the Word of God and call forth "dry bones" to come back to life, our action to declare God's Word aloud activates the spirit realm. Why? Because God breathed life into Scripture, activating its power to work in our lives.

> All Scripture is *breathed out by God* and profitable for teaching, for reproof, for correction, and for training in righteousness, that the man of God may be complete, equipped for every good work.
> —2 Timothy 3:16–17, ESV, emphasis added

When we speak God's Word, our act of faith releases His power to breathe life into our circumstances.

SOUL

Regardless of your belief system (or lack thereof, because even atheists believe in something although they don't believe in deities), your words have the power to bring death or life.

> The tongue can bring death or life;
> those who love to talk will reap the
> consequences.
> —Proverbs 18:21, NLT

The choice is yours. You can speak life into a circumstance and with the very same tongue curse people, causing irreparable damage to that individual's spirit. In the same way your words impact others, your self-proclaimed words also impact your life—positively and negatively.

I heard a sermon by Pastor Robert Morris of Gateway Church in Dallas describing how the breath of God operates in our lives. He said it brings strength, order, understanding, and life.

- **S**trength
- **O**rder
- **U**nderstanding
- **L**ife

Pastor Morris didn't create this acronym when teaching about these characteristics, but as I was studying the Word, God gave me insight into this teaching. The breath of God breathes new life into our dead **SOUL**s. Let's be vigilant to guard what rolls off our tongues.

We should make an effort to breathe life into others and situations, and call forth those things that are not as though they are already done. (See Romans 4:16–22, especially verse 17.)

As part of God's restoration process, He *strengthens* our "bones" by attaching sinews and muscles to them. We are responsible for building spiritual muscles by continuing to exercise our faith and fulfill our purpose.

Next, God brings *order* to our lives because He is a God of order, not the author of confusion. Once He brings order out of the chaos in our lives, He provides us with *understanding*—that is, godly wisdom.

The Word says, "Wisdom is the principal thing; therefore get wisdom: and with all thy getting get understanding" (Prov. 4:7, KJV). In order to continue to build upon what God has started in our lives, we need to walk in godly wisdom to avoid falling back into old habits and lifestyle.

Finally, having ordered our steps and as we continue to gain spiritual wisdom, He breathes new *life* into our dreams and hopes that have withered to an anorexic state during our wilderness experience. The wilderness is never meant to be a permanent state, but rather a place of preparation.

> *Don't let anyone rob you
> of your imagination, your
> creativity, or your curiosity.
> Go on and do all you can
> with it, and make it the life
> you want to live.*
> —Mae Jemison

Sometimes, we are set in these abandoned and forgotten about places so God can use us to breathe life and bring order from chaos and dysfunction. God has anointed our hands to build, and God has given us the grace to help others build. The gifts, talents, and abilities that He has placed inside of us are not for our self-exaltation—they are to be used to glorify God.

God uses your gifts to build up the old and breathe life into the worn-down things. God has given you the authority to rebuild and to speak life into stagnant areas.

Ezekiel said, "The hand of the Lord was upon me, and carried me out in the spirit of the Lord, and set me down in the midst of the valley which was full of bones" (Ezek. 37:1, KJV). God sent him to the valley of dry bones. Oftentimes, God places us in dead, dry, dark places. Our mandate as His children is to be light and speak life into the dead, dry, defeated, and forgotten things. We are to say what God says concerning the circumstance.

In this season, and in every season, it is important to be led by God in everything you say and do. The hand of the Lord was upon Ezekiel, and God's hand is upon you. God will carry you through the valley. Even though dry bones may surround you, don't be discouraged by what you see. God sent you where you are so He could use you to do something miraculous for His glory.

Come Closer

We also use our "god-killer" through an active prayer life. When we pray in agreement with the will of God and verbally declare His Word, releasing it into the atmosphere, the Word is activated according to our faith. Ephesians 6:18 tells us to "pray in the Spirit on all occasions with all kinds of prayers and requests. With this in mind, be alert and always keep on praying for all the Lord's people."

> *Battle prayers are a threat to your enemy because he knows how dangerous you can be to his tactics when faith arises within you.*

Sometimes we pray in silence, sometimes we pray in our heavenly language, and sometimes we pray in our native language. But prayer is activating what God's Word says by verbally declaring it in our environment and over our lives.

> *Prayer is activating what God's Word says by verbally declaring it in our environment and over our lives.*

For example, God challenged me during this writing process to raise the quality of my prayer life, to move beyond superficial prayers of protection and other things He already promised to do. I began searching for scriptures to memorize and come into agreement with by declaring them aloud during my prayer time. He encouraged me to ask Him for more—to push beyond the current level of my faith and ask and believe Him for the impossible. He challenged me to trust Him to deliver on what I ask, make my request according to His Word, and have faith that He will come through.

When I taught Sunday school to small children and would try to get them to pay attention, I'd place my index finger over my lips and say, "*Shhh!* Inside voices, everyone. Use your inside voices, please." But they were usually too jacked up from the sugary drinks we served them with tiny cups of goldfish crackers to listen. What a challenge!

Often in Christian circles, we reference the inner voice of the Holy Spirit as that "still, small voice" guiding us in the way we should go, if we listen. But God has an outside voice, and He's not afraid to use it.

In Mark 4:35–41, we find Jesus asleep on a boat in the middle of a storm. His disciples are panicking because the boat is filling up with water. But Jesus isn't fazed by the circumstances; He's peacefully resting. Then Jesus *speaks to the wind and waves, "Peace! Be still."* With one command, He calms the sea. That same commanding authority calms the storms in our lives and quiets our fears.

But when God wants to be heard, when what He has to say is too important to miss, He often speaks at a hearing level just above a whisper. It's that still, small voice. Why does He do this? When someone whispers, you have to draw closer to the person to hear what is being said. The distance between the two of you narrows, creating greater intimacy than standing feet apart.

Nobody is probably more familiar with the quietness of God's voice than Elijah, an Old Testament prophet. Elijah had taken on the prophets of Baal in a bold confrontation on Mount Carmel. God literally sent fire from heaven and burned up the offering Eli-

The god-Killer

jah set out. But after Elijah had such an incredible mountaintop experience, the wicked queen Jezebel threatened Elijah's life, and he ran in fear. Jezebel drove Elijah into a wilderness experience. Depressed, suicidal, and on the run, Elijah felt he couldn't take life anymore. (See 1 Kings 19:3–4.) But it was in this desperate time that Elijah found himself most comforted by God's care and presence.

After fleeing Jezebel, Elijah rested under a broom tree, and as he was sleeping, an angel touched him and said, "Get up and eat!" Elijah looked around, and beside his head was some bread baked on hot stones and a jar of water.

So he got up and ate and drank, and the food gave him enough strength to travel forty days and forty nights to Mount Sinai, the mountain of God. There he arrived at a cave, where he spent the night.

> But the Lord said to him, "What are you doing here, Elijah?"
>
> Elijah replied, "I have zealously served the Lord God Almighty. But the people of Israel have broken their covenant with you, torn down your altars, and killed every one of your prophets. I am the only one left, and now they are trying to kill me, too."
>
> —1 Kings 19:9–10, NLT

What happened next is nothing short of miraculous. God told Elijah to go out and stand before Him on the mountain. A mighty, rushing wind passed by Elijah that blasted the rocks away, but the Lord wasn't in the wind. After that, there was an earthquake, but He wasn't speaking to him through that either. Then after the earthquake, there was a fire, but that's not what God uses to capture Elijah's attention either.

> And after the fire there was the sound of a gentle whisper. When Elijah heard it, he wrapped his face in his cloak and went out and stood at the entrance of the cave.
> —1 Kings 19:12–13, NLT

Elijah went from a mountaintop experience to a wilderness experience just like that. My pastor has a saying that you're either in a storm, just coming out of a storm, or about to enter a storm. Life isn't always sunshine and rainbows. But what we can take away from Elijah's experience is that God is always closest to us when we think we least deserve His love. He's patient with us and loves us through everything—the good, the bad, and the ugly.

This is why God so often speaks in whispers. When someone speaks in a whisper, you have to get very close to hear. In fact, you have to put your ear near the person's mouth. We lean toward a whisper, and that's what God wants. The goal of hearing the heavenly Father's voice isn't just to hear His voice; it's to experience intimacy with Him. He speaks in a whisper because He wants to be as close to us as is divinely possible! He loves us—and likes us—that much.

> *Your deepest need becomes your greatest gift when it drives you to depend on God.*
> *—Pastor Shaddy Soliman*

Aren't you grateful for a gentle God? He could intimidate us with His outside voice, but instead He woos us with a whisper. And His whisper is the very breath of life.

Friedrich Nietzsche is often quoted as saying, "Those who were seen dancing were thought to be insane by those who could not hear the music." That is certainly true of those who walk to the beat of God's drum. When you take your cues from the Holy Spirit, you'll do some things that will make people think you're crazy. So be it. What do you care what people think so long as you know you're doing exactly what God has placed in your heart to do?

What matters most is what God thinks about you, and He thinks the world of you! Obey the whisper and see what God does, because nothing has the potential to change your life like the whisper of God. Nothing will determine your destiny more than your ability to hear His still, small voice. That's how God-sized dreams are birthed. That's how miracles happen.

Regardless of how the circumstance looks, keep on praying! Eventually that circumstance will shift. Even though we may see a significant breakthrough in someone's life, that person may still need to be lifted up in prayer. There used to be bumper stickers and bracelets reminding Christians to **PUSH** (Pray Until Something Happens). I've been feeling impressed lately that even though we may see evidence of God moving, we need to keep pressing on in prayer. We need to remember the acronym **PAST**—and "Pray After Someone Turns" also!

The Hand of the Lord Is Upon You

This chapter opened with how Wonder Woman wielded her sword at the enemy, only to realize that the true weapon was not the sword itself. The true weapon was the power that lay within her. What's the weakness in that, you may ask? The weakness is the failure to recognize that she carried the weapon within her all along. It wasn't a tangible object that would destroy her enemy; she was the god-killer. Like Wonder

Woman, we sometimes allow the sword of the Spirit—the Word of God—to lie dormant on the inside of us rather than wielding it to engage in warfare with our enemy and defeat him. If we mediate on Scripture and pray the Word aloud, God breathes life into the situation. And when the Word is released through a prayer of faith, it becomes a powerful weapon.

God's Word is living and active, sharper than any two-edged sword (Heb. 4:12). If we yield to the Word, it searches our hearts and cuts out the evil intentions that lie within it.

The hand of God is with you to transform cultures and ignite environments. Speak life into your workplace, over your family, into long-forgotten dreams, visions, and goals. Stay the course and speak life to the valley of dry bones. *Speak.* Say what God is telling you to say. Restore hope in others. Help others fulfill their dreams before fulfilling your own and see if maybe God won't shower you with blessings for being selfless. It's time to build. It's time for you to step into your purpose.

Information Warfare Plan

As you meditate on this week's scriptures, think about the ways in which the Word of God has been activated to release miracles in your life.

Recommended Daily Scriptures:

- Day 1: Matthew 6:9–15
- Day 2: Romans 8:24–28
- Day 3: Daniel 6:8–28
- Day 4: Daniel 10:7–15
- Day 5: Luke 18:1–8
- Day 6: Mark 11:24
- Day 7: Luke 5:16

Finally, be strong in the Lord and in his mighty power.
—Ephesians 6:10

Conclusion

Will You Answer the Call?

Wonder Woman makes a choice to stay in the world of men and not return to her home, the island of Themyscira. She made a conscious decision to answer the call of her heart. Now that you possess the knowledge of your God-given weapons and powers, it is time for you to rise up and answer the call to become a change agent within your sphere of influence. You are not called to sit on the sidelines. Go and pay it forward by discipling others.

That calling you have is not so God will become part of your story; it's so you will become part of *His*. If you have a conviction in your heart to influence those around you, then it doesn't matter who is for or against you, because God already said He is always for you (Rom. 8:31). Answering the call is about who and what you stand for. You are not just a woman living under authority—you are a woman who has authority and walks in it.

Please don't go and twist what I'm saying here. This isn't about feminism or flexing your position as a woman in society. The #MeToo movement started with the right intention, but unfortunately some have pushed the movement's pendulum too far in the other direction. When I say you have authority and should walk in it, I'm talking about you having been given a responsibility to be a person of influence in the world.

The question you must ask yourself is, Will I live consumed with worry about who is for or against me, or will I live consumed with the One I am for? Am I making my mark and fulfilling some humanistic purpose, or is God making His mark through me?

As the Lord directs you to embrace your calling and respond to the stirring in your heart for His destiny and purpose for you, I believe you will develop a divine urgency and sense of responsibility for doing things greater than you could in your own strength. I believe you will begin to see yourself as a woman of influence, conviction, and power.

There is a divinely inspired cry coming out of the hearts of women, declaring, "The enemy can't have my loved ones or my inheritance as a daughter of the King. Not on *my* watch!" The passion and righteous indignation of the Lord is arising in the hearts of women to take up the spiritual weapons we've been given to touch heaven and bring reformation on the earth.

Recommended Resources

My hope and prayer are that this book has somehow influenced you in a positive way and encouraged you to make the changes needed to fulfill your purpose. If this book has helped you in any way, I'd love to hear from you.

Instagram: @lillianlaitman
Facebook: @LillianlaitmanFB

www.lillianlaitman.com

If this book has challenged what you believe about God and you'd like to learn more about growing in your faith, here are some resources you may find helpful.

Churches and Ministries

- Lake Mary Church / http://lakemarychurch.com
- Every Nation Churches and Ministries / https://www.everynation.org

Discipleship Resources:

- The God Test / www.thegodtest.org
- *God's Not Dead* film

About the Author

Lillian Laitman has won numerous awards as an editor and served as a trusted advisor to bestselling authors in Christian and business leadership over her 25-plus-year publishing career.

Her greatest passion, however, is to help all women discover their uniqueness and walk in their purpose. In 2020, she launched her longtime vision to establish WoW Media, which has a mission to empower people to fulfill their God-given purpose, become influencers, and have a lasting, positive impact on their world.

Lillian has a bachelor's degree in English from the University of Central Florida and a master's degree in publishing from George Washington University. Lillian's happiest place on Earth is not the "Mouse's House" but the beach. When she's not working on a book project, she loves spending time with family and close friends. She enjoys traveling and most water sports like kayaking, fishing, and boating. She resides in the Central Florida area with her two children and rescue basset hound mix, Maxie.

Endnotes

Introduction

1. Bible Hub, s.v. "kathairesis," accessed April 5, 2020, https://biblehub.com/greek/2506.htm.

2. Sheila E. Widnall and Ronald R. Fogelman, "Cornerstones of Information Warfare," 1997, accessed December 26, 2019, http://www.iwar.org.uk/iwar/resources/usaf/iw/corner.html.

Chapter 1

1. Joe Burgett, "15 Weaknesses You Didn't Know Wonder Woman Had," ScreenRant.com, May 18, 2017, https://screenrant.com/wonder-woman-biggest-weakness-didnt-know-trivia/; Michael Graff, "15 Things You Didn't know About Wonder Woman's Sword and Shield," ScreenRant.com, June 15, 2017, https://screenrant.com/wonder-woman-sword-shield-trivia-facts-godkiler/.

2. Michael Graff, "15 Things You Didn't know About Wonder Woman's Sword and Shield."

3. Michael Graff, "15 Things You Didn't know About Wonder Woman's Sword and Shield."

Chapter 2

1. Joe Burgett, 15 Weaknesses You Didn't Know Wonder Woman Had," ScreenRant.com, May 18, 2017, https://screenrant.com/wonder-woman-biggest-weakness-didnt-know-trivia/

Chapter 3

1. Joe Burgett, "15 Weaknesses You Didn't Know Wonder Woman Had"; see also Kofi Outlaw, "Wonder Woman's Movie Powers & Abilities Explained," ComicBook.com, November 9, 2017, https://comicbook.com/dc/2017/06/03/wonder-woman-movie-powers-abilities-dceu/.

2. "Wonder Woman's Bracelets" Wikipedia, accessed April 4, 2020, https://en.wikipedia.org/wiki/Wonder_Woman%27s_bracelets.

3. *Merriam-Webster.com, s.v. "never," accessed April 5, 2020, https://www.merriam-webster.com/dictionary/never.*

4. "The Power of Forgiveness," Harvard Health Publishing May 2019, https://www.health.harvard.edu/mind-and-mood/the-power-of-forgiveness.

5. Blue Letter Bible, s.v. *"diabolos,"* accessed December 28, 2019, *https://www.blueletterbible.org/lang/Lexicon/Lexicon.cfm?strongs=G1228&t=KJV.*

Chapter 4

1. Michael Graff, "15 Things You Didn't know About Wonder Woman's Sword and Shield."

Chapter 5

1. Gem Rock Auctions.com, "The Truth about Chocolate Diamonds." Accessed April 15, 2020. https://www.gemrockauctions.com/learn/did-you-know/the-truth-chocolate-diamonds.

2. Gem Rock Auctions.com, "The Truth about Chocolate Diamonds." Accessed April 15, 2020. https://www.gemrockauctions.com/learn/did-you-know/the-truth-chocolate-diamonds.

3. Blue Letter Bible, s.v. *"anakainoō,"* accessed April 5, 2020, https://www.blueletterbible.org/lang/Lexicon/Lexicon.cfm?strongs=G341&t=KJV.

Chapter 6

1. *McGraw-Hill Dictionary of American Idioms and Phrasal Verbs*, s.v. "old battle-axe," accessed April 5, 2020, https://idioms.thefreedictionary.com/old+battle-axe.

2. Dave Johnson, "Armor of God: Helmet of Salvation," Church of God, Worldwide Association, accessed December 29, 2019, https://lifehopeandtruth.com/change/christian-conversion/armor-of-god/helmet-of-salvation/.

3. Rick Renner, "The Helmet of Salvation," Rick Renner Ministries, August 4, 2016, https://renner.org/the-helmet-of-salvation/.

4. Chelsea Gomez, "An unhealed person can find offense in pretty much anything someone else does." Twitter, May 28, 2019, https://twitter.com/ChelseaGomez42/status/1133564255628873730.

5. Blue Letter Bible, s.v. *"peripoiēsis," accessed April 5, 2020, https://www.blueletterbible.org/lang/Lexicon/Lexicon.cfm?strongs=G4047&t=KJV.*

Chapter 7

1. Michael Graff, "15 Things You Didn't know About Wonder Woman's Sword and Shield."

2. "Those Who Dance Are Considered Insane by Those Who Can't Hear the Music," Quote Investigator, accessed April 5, 2020, https://quoteinvestigator.com/2012/06/05/dance-insane/.

www.ingramcontent.com/pod-product-compliance
Lightning Source LLC
Chambersburg PA
CBHW071347080526
44587CB00017B/3003